INTRODUCING
CHINESE CASSEROLE COOKERY

INTRODUCING
CHINESE
CASSEROLE
COOKERY

LILAH KAN
EDITED BY HELEN WITTY

WORKMAN PUBLISHING, NEW YORK

With special thanks to Helen Scott-Harman

Library of Congress Cataloging in Publication Data
Kan, Lilah.
    Introducing Chinese casserole cookery.
    Includes index.
    1. Cookery, Chinese. 2. Casserole cookery.
I. Witty, Helen. II. Title.
TX724.5.C5K314   641.8'21   78-7117
ISBN 0-89480-047-7
ISBN 0-89480-048-5 pbk.

Jacket and book design: Charles Kreloff
Jacket and book photography: Jerry Darvin

Workman Publishing Company, Inc.
1 West 39th Street
New York, New York 10018

Manufactured in the United States of America
First printing November 1978

10   9   8   7   6   5   4   3   2

For my mother, Wei Har Tom Kan,
and my sons, Jeremy and Jonathan Spear

CONTENTS

PORK

LAMB

SEAFOOD

DUCK, SQUAB, CORNISH HENS, AND TURKEY

COMBINATION POTS

RICE-BASED CASSEROLES AND CONGEE

INTRODUCING CHINESE CASSEROLE COOKERY

Chinese casserole cookery? Absolutely. Stove-top casserole dishes, a very ancient and authentic part of Chinese cuisine, have been gathered in this cookbook — the first of its kind — as a direct result of the renewal of trade and travel between the United States and China. Pots and politics have come together, and cooks are the winners.

The long hiatus in trade relations between the two countries after World War II prevented Americans, increasingly interested in and adept at Oriental cooking, from discovering the characteristic Chinese earthenware casseroles or learning how the Chinese cook with them. Americans who liked to cook with Chinese equipment were limited essentially to the wok and the steamer. But with the recipes in this book and any type of casserole, anyone fond of Chinese cooking can add countless new dishes to his or her repertoire.

To most Westerners, Chinese cooking is stir-frying. Yet, in texts surviving from the Chou dynasty (1124 to 249 B.C.), the technique of stir-frying is not mentioned; whereas boiling, steaming, roasting, and simmering-stewing are. Keng, a meat soup or stew, was the most common type of food cooked during that period. The dominance of keng was confirmed by an important archaeological discovery made near Ch'ang-sha in Hunan in 1972. The body of a woman, probably the wife of the first marquis of Tai, who reigned from 193 to 186 B.C., was found in remarkably well-preserved condition. In her tomb, the archaeologists found foodstuffs that give a good picture of Han dynasty cuisine and over 300 bamboo slips itemizing foods, seasonings, and cooking methods (a royal cookbook?). Those slips clearly indicate that keng was the primary main dish in China from antiquity to the Han period (206 B.C. to A.D. 220). Keng was the precursor of the technique known today as red-cooking (simmering the food in a mixture of black soy sauce, wine, and various condiments that gives the food a dark brown color).

In China, there is a long tradition of restaurants that feature casserole cooking. Sha Kuo Chu ("Home of the Earthen-Pot Casserole") in Peking was established in the 1700s and is famous for its huge earthenware casserole, four feet in diameter, in which pork is cooked. But in the United States, there are few restaurants, even in San Francisco and New York, that feature what they call clay pot cooking or village home-style cooking. Other restaurants include a few casserole dishes on their otherwise conventional menus, dishes such as a fish head casserole, a rice pot with meat and vegetables cooked on top of the rice, or a combination pot.

Most Americans have learned about Chinese food from eating in Chinese restaurants in the United States, not from family-style Chinese home cooking. And because stir-frying is the major restaurant cooking technique here, Americans have concluded that stir-frying is the only way to cook Chinese. But in Chinese homes, stewed or simmered dishes are frequently served along with a soup, a stir-fried or steamed dish, and rice for a meal that offers an interesting variety of tastes and textures. The recipes in this book will fit equally well into an American meal that includes rice or noodles, a green vegetable, and perhaps a mixed salad.

There is no single school of Chinese casserole cookery; foods from every culinary region of China can be prepared in these vessels. With the imaginativeness and flexibility typical of the many cuisines of China, the casserole may hold a sizable cut of pork, beef, or lamb braised with vegetables or simmered in a sauce; an attractive mélange of seafood, meats, and vegetables; cellophane noodles with Chinese sausages or with minced beef or pork; subtly sauced chicken wings; many kinds of soupy pots; a ragoût Chinois of beef or lamb or a variety meat such as oxtails; a whole braised chicken or duck or even a small turkey; spareribs in a sauce enlivened with Chinese spicing; meatballs layered with cabbage to make lions' heads (the cabbage forms the manes); or congee (jook), a rice gruel served with a fascinating variety of condiments and accompaniments. Some dishes have a very soupy consistency; others are braised in a sauce that has body. The style depends on the inclination and inventiveness of the individual chef. In short, a Chinese casserole can be almost any dish that requires more than a very short spell of stir-frying over the fire or any dish not meant to be deep-fried, steamed, or oven-roasted.

Sauce is as important to Chinese cookery as it is to the French. When a new Chinese restaurant opens, other Chinese restaurateurs traditionally send some of their master sauce to the new venture for good luck. This master sauce is, in fact, the braising sauce called for in most of the recipes in this book. It is a combination of soy sauce, wine, and spices and is used to simmer or stew meats and vegetables. Leftover braising liquid can be frozen and reused for similar foods. Just take care to save your sauce from the clean-up efforts of a zealous helper or dishwasher.

If you enjoy entertaining, you will find the recipes in this book a boon. Many of my cooking students have described the hysteria that seizes them when cooking several stir-fried dishes. There are so many things to do — all at the same time. They are captives of their kitchens until all the dishes are cooked. By the time they arrive at the dinner table, they are exhausted, the stove is a mess, and most of the food has already been devoured by the appreciative guests. But one or two casserole dishes on the menu will ease the burden of frantic last-minute cooking and allow the host or hostess to spend more time enjoying the company of the guests.

This book supplies more than recipes; it includes everything the cook needs to know to cook casseroles Chinese style. The preparation techniques are easy to master. They are described in text and in step-by-step photographs. Many traditional imported ingredients are called for in these recipes. They are increasingly abundant in supermarkets — witness the wide availability of good imported soy sauce. Fresh ginger root, following the path of once-scarce garlic, is fast becoming a greengrocer's staple in many places.

This book will introduce you to an important form of traditional Chinese family-style cooking. The recipes are intended as guides for you to follow — not slavishly but with imagination. Adjust, add, substitute, or eliminate ingredients according to your own tastes. One of the reasons for the greatness of the cuisine of one-quarter of the world's population is that it is a cuisine of invention, flexibility, and variation that uses whatever is available locally and seasonally. If a totally new food were to appear tomorrow, Chinese cooks would quickly make use of it in completely new but also thoroughly Chinese ways.

You will have both fun and good eating with this style of cooking. Enjoy it.

CASSEROLES

Casseroles are among the most ancient of cooking vessels. It is possible that the first earthenware pot evolved from the technique of encasing fowl or small animals in wet clay and then baking them over hot stones and ashes. By the time the food was cooked, the mud or clay had hardened. It was then broken and removed, pulling the feather or fur off the animal in the process. (Beggar's Chicken, a well-known Chinese dish, still uses this method.) At some point, someone must have gotten the idea of making a permanent receptacle that could be used over and over again. This is pure speculation, of course, but it is not really all that unlikely.

The archaeological dig at Ch'ang-sha revealed that the major utensils of the Han period were the <u>fu</u> (cauldron) and the <u>tseng</u> (steamer). Most were made of clay, although some iron and bronze utensils were also found. It seems that the <u>tseng</u>, which held grain, was placed on top of the <u>fu</u>, a technique that saved fuel and paired the basic foods of that period, stew and grain.

Cuisines all over the world and throughout history have used earthenware vessels for long-simmered dishes. Now a Chinese utensil that is new to Americans has begun to appear in grocery and housewares stores in major Chinatowns: a clay pot with coarse, sandy-textured beige exterior (with a sooty streak here or there, no doubt from the kiln) and a dark brown, smoothly glazed interior. (The glaze is lead-free and perfectly safe for cooking.) Most of these pots are caged in a network of wire that helps to protect the somewhat fragile earthenware.

This pot comes in three basic shapes and various sizes. The most common shape is a squat casserole with sloping sides; a flared, hollow handle; and a lid that may or may not be glazed dark brown on the outside. Some of the lids have two little loops through which a strand of

wire can be threaded to make a handle. This type of casserole is most commonly used by the Chinese restaurants that specialize in clay pot cooking. It comes in sizes to serve one, two, four or many more.

The second clay pot shape is tall and bulbous. These pots have unglazed lids topped with a small clay knob that has a steam hole in it. They are usually used for soups or congee, and they hold 4 quarts or more.

The most modern-looking clay pot is also squat and has two handles, but it has a smoother-textured exterior than the other types. It is interchangeable with the more common squat casserole.

Some Chinese cookbooks have included pictures of these casseroles, but most do not explain how they are used. Readers have been left to wonder whether these pots can be put over gas or electric heat or whether they can be used only in the oven. My mother remembers such casseroles well and says they were much used during the winters; they were simply placed on top of the charcoal braziers used to heat the house. (Ovens are rare in China.) Clay pots can be placed directly over gas or electric heat. They can, of course, be put in the oven; but frankly, I feel that this is a waste of fuel. That is why all the recipes in this book call for top-of-the-stove cooking at very low temperatures.

Sandy pots are somewhat porous and will sweat a little because of condensation until they have been seasoned by repeated use. But there is a way to reduce or even eliminate this temporary problem. In the course of my research for this book, I came across a pamphlet printed in England at the turn of the century (that certainly illustrates the long and widespread popularity of earthenware casseroles) listing instructions for preparing earthenware casseroles for use the very first time.

Here is what you should do: Begin by rubbing the outside

surface of the pot, the part that comes into contact with the heat source, with a cut clove of garlic or a shallot until the entire bottom surface is darkened and looks moist. (The oil is what does this.) Then fill the pot with water, add a generous pinch of salt, place the pot over low heat, and gradually bring the water to a boil. The booklet's author recommends using an asbestos pad to temper the heat even more effectively. Let the water boil for a few minutes; then remove the pot from the heat. Let the casserole cool, empty the water, and dry the pot thoroughly. Your clay pot is now ready for use.

Here are two important notes of caution: <u>Never</u> place an empty clay pot on the heat; there should always be liquid in the pot to prevent it from cracking. <u>Never</u> place a hot casserole on a damp or cold surface or bring it into contact with water until it has cooled; the combination of hot pot and wet or cold surface will crack the pot.

If you purchase a Chinese clay pot, check it for leaks. Most stores will be happy to do this for you. They will float the pot in water to see if any water seeps through to the interior, or fill the pot with water and place it on dry newspapers to see if any water leaks out.

Chinese earthenware casseroles are inexpensive, and their simplicity is very attractive. Their texture, which has earned them the name <u>sandy pots</u>, allows slow transmission of heat, which makes them ideal stew pots. And, of course, they have the appeal of authenticity. Undoubtedly, they will gain in popularity and be easier to obtain.

However, it most certainly is <u>not</u> essential to have a clay pot in order to cook Chinese casseroles, just as it is not necessary to have a wok to stir-fry. Enameled or plain cast-iron casseroles with lids will do just as well; the only   requirement is that the casserole must be flameproof. You <u>can</u> learn and enjoy Chinese casserole cookery using equipment that you already have; the following photographs provide a few suggestions.

This Descoware oval enameled cast-iron casserole was manufactured by a Belgian firm that is now out of business. It is the author's favorite and has given many years of good use. You no doubt have your own favorite casserole. If it is not one of the types shown in this section, by all means use it anyway.

Danish-manufactured Copco casseroles are made of enameled cast iron. They come in 1½- to 7-quart capacities and are available in a variety of colors.

Magnalite oval roasters, of cast magnesium-aluminum alloy, are manufactured in the United States and are widely available. These pots are described by their length or by the weight of the fowl the pot will hold, rather than by capacity in quarts.

Corning Ware® casseroles are square and made of white glass with clear glass lids. They come in 1-, 1½, 2-, 3-, and 5-quart capacities. The manufacturer guarantees that they can be used for top-of-the-stove cooking.

Many companies manufacture aluminum casseroles covered with patterned enamel. This particular shape usually comes in a 4- or 5-quart capacity. They are readily available in a wide variety of designs.

Cast-iron Dutch ovens manufactured by Wagner or Griswold come in capacities of 3 to 7 quarts. The interior is smooth and glazed dark brown, the texture of the exterior is rough but not so coarse as the Chinese clay pots.

PREPARATION TECHNIQUES

Preparation and organization are necessary to efficient cooking, and the key to preparation lies in the mastery of certain kitchen skills. I believe it was Martha Graham who said that to become an artist, one must study and master technique. Of course, we cannot all be artists in the kitchen, but we <u>can</u> learn methods that will make cooking easier and more enjoyable.

From my years as a cooking instructor, I know I must anticipate the insecurities that people experience when learning about a cuisine that is new to them. Some of the procedures called for in this book may seem exotic and difficult to you, but they are really quite simple.

The photographs that follow take you through these techniques step by step. All you need is a little practice to become an old hand at the methods used by veteran Chinese chefs.

The only unusual tool that you will need for the following Chinese casserole cookery techniques is the Chinese cleaver. At first, my cooking students find it a formidable instrument, but they soon realize that it is indispensable for all types of food preparation. (It is even rumored that Julia Child uses a Chinese cleaver rather than a French chef's knife.) The Chinese cleaver looks frightening, and if it is carelessly used, it <u>can</u> cause damage. But if the cleaver is used with care and respect, it can take preparation work out of the realm of chores and into the area of delight and pride. It is one kitchen instrument I cannot do without. I always take one with me whenever friends invite me to spend a weekend in the country or at the beach ("Have cleaver, will travel"). The reputation of the Chinese cleaver as an all-purpose tool in <u>any</u> kitchen has spread to the extent that an

American cutlery firm now produces an excellent cleaver with a fine edge that is easily sharpened; it is sold in cutlery shops throughout the country.

When I cooked kosher Chinese food at the Ramada Continental Hotel in Tel Aviv, I always had to hide the Chinese cleavers I brought with me because the Israeli cooks found them so useful for chopping, mincing, dicing, and slicing meats and vegetables that they were forever borrowing them and forgetting to return them.

A Chinese cleaver is more versatile than a regular knife, and its usefulness is not confined to mere cutting. Sliced meat and vegetables can be transferred to a mixing bowl or casserole by sliding the pieces onto the cleaver (page 27). You can also use the broad blade of the cleaver to flatten ginger slices, chicken breasts, veal scallops, or medallions of pork. The handle can be used as a pestle to mash the salted black beans called for in a number of recipes in this book. If you have two cleavers, you can chop meat to hamburger or even consistency: Hold a cleaver in each hand with the blades parallel and about 2 inches apart, and mince the meat with alternating up-down strokes. You will be finished in a surprisingly short period of time. (Never raise one cleaver higher than the other; if you do, you may not maintain the parallel position, and you will hit one blade with the other.)

One chore for which you will find the Chinese cleaver invaluable is cutting a chicken into frying (or even smaller) pieces — a technique that every cook should know. This skill can be acquired with patience and good will. The photographs in this chapter show how I hack a chicken into small pieces. You can also use this technique to cut a cooked whole chicken or a raw or cooked duck into small pieces.

The Chinese cleaver is also excellent for slicing onions, a chore that some cooks find tedious. If you patiently practice the methods shown here, it will become easier to do. Necessity made me become a master onion slicer. As a chef in Chinese and French restaurants, I often had to slice over 10 pounds of onions a day, so I learned to do it <u>fast.</u> I can even slice onions with my eyes closed (<u>not</u> a recommended technique), although I only do it when I want to showboat. Jack Gelber, the playwright and director, once brought actor Randall Duk Kim to my house so that I could show Randy the proper way to cut vegetables with a Chinese cleaver for a scene in a play Jack was directing at the American Place Theatre. Jack wanted not only authenticity but also an actor with uncut hands.

Of course, there are some things that you cannot use the medium-weight Chinese cleaver for because you might damage the blade. The cleaver is perfect for slicing, trimming, and hacking, but it will not cut through heavy bone. You can buy a heavy cleaver for heavy-duty chopping.

All the sparerib recipes (except Chinese-Style Spareribs and Sauerkraut) call for the ribs to be cut into 2-inch pieces. This is best done by a butcher, who will use a meat saw or heavy cleaver; supermarket butchers are often willing to do the job, even though the ribs are already packaged as an intact rack. However, you can do the job yourself with a heavy meat cleaver.

Another thing that my students tend to be in awe of is the mystique of cooking Chinese-style rice. The process is actually very simple. The underlying principle is that the rice grains must be washed and rinsed thoroughly to get rid of excess starch; that keeps the cooked rice from being gummy. When the water runs clear, the rice is ready to cook. One of my household chores as a child was to wash the dinner rice for eleven people, and I made a game of getting the water <u>crystal</u> clear. The results are well worth the little extra time you will spend in preparation.

Just as it is important to get rid of excess starch in cooking rice, it is also necessary to render excess fat from a duck before it is cooked in a casserole. I have devised a method that removes almost 1 cup of fat and that gives the duck a rich brown color. The procedure is simple: Hot salt in a hot skillet draws out the subcutaneous fat, and the duck begins to brown in its own fat. (I got the idea for this technique when I had read about a similar method used for pan-frying steaks and hamburgers in a cookbook by James Beard and in an article in the <u>New York Times</u> by Mimi Sheraton.)

There is one technique given here that is <u>not</u> as simple as it looks: making egg-pouch dumplings. As with crêpes, you may find yourself throwing out the first few until you have made the necessary temperature adjustments and found out just how much oil you need, how much egg to pour into the pan, and how much filling mixture to place on top of the egg without making an overstuffed or a skimpy dumpling.

Do not be discouraged if your first efforts are failures. In making dumplings, as in mastering all the techniques shown here, practice <u>does</u> make perfect — and makes for perfect results.

PREPARING THE CASSEROLE

1. Wash the head of lettuce, drain it, and discard any wilted leaves. Peel off as many leaves as necessary to line the bottom and sides of the casserole. Begin by arranging the lettuce leaves along the sides.

2. Fill in the bottom, pressing the leaves flat. (Of course, the number of leaves will vary with the size of the casserole.)

3. If onions are called for in the preparation of the casserole, slice them (see page 26) before lining the casserole. Then scoop the pieces up with the end of the cleaver, and sprinkle them on top of the lettuce.

SLICING ONIONS

1. Cut off the top and root end of the onion. Note how the cleaver is held: The forefinger extends slightly along the blade, the thumb slightly beyond the handle; the other three fingers curl around the handle. The opposite hand holds the onion firmly. The forefinger and middle finger are tucked under to get the fingertips (<u>not</u> the secret ingredient) out of the way; the bent knuckles act as a cutting guide.

2. Place the onion on one of its cut ends, and slice it in half. Never raise the cleaver higher than the knuckles. For control and balance, let the weight of the cleaver work for you. Cut with the middle section of the blade.

3. Peel the skin off both onion halves. (Onions are easier to peel after they have been cut in half.)

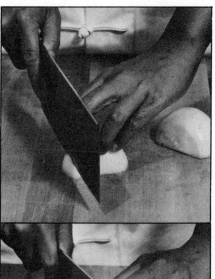

4. Place the onion half on the cutting surface, cut side down, and slice the onion <u>along</u> the grain (not across it).

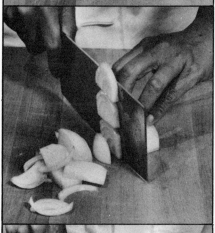

5. As you slice the onion, you will notice that the moisture of the cut slices causes them to cling to the side of the blade and ride up the blade, pushing the top slice off and onto a pile on the side. When most of the onion is cut and the remaining section rests on a narrow base, flip it onto its wider cut side, and continue to slice.

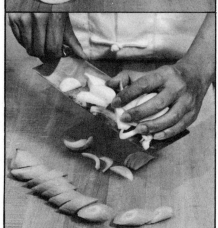

6. Carefully scoop up the slices with the end of the cleaver. (Avoid contact with the edge so that you do not cut yourself.) Transfer the onions to the casserole if it is being lined with lettuce and onion slices (page 25), or to a plate or bowl until you need them for the recipe. Note that a trimmed and peeled carrot has been sliced diagonally, using the same technique. (Slicing on the diagonal exposes a larger cut surface for more even cooking.)

COOKING RICE CHINESE STYLE

1. Put the long-grain rice in a pot or casserole large enough to hold triple the amount of raw rice (1 cup of raw rice more than doubles when cooked), and fill the pot with cold water.

2. Stir the rice with your hand. The water will be cloudy. Washing the rice gets rid of excess starch and prevents the cooked rice from being gummy.

3. Pour the water out of the pot slowly and carefully, holding your free hand under the edge of the pot to catch any rice grains.

4. Stir the drained rice to loosen more starch. Then repeat steps 1, 2, and 3 until the water runs crystal clear.

5. Place the tip of your thumb on top of the rice. Pour in cold water. The water should reach almost to the first knuckle (about ¾ inch from the top of the rice).

6. Cover the pot, and place it over high heat. When the water comes to a violent boil, immediately reduce the heat to the lowest setting. Do not peek, stir, or add salt or butter. The rice will be done in 20 to 25 minutes. If you use a heavy-bottomed pot, the rice can stay over very low heat for as long as 1 hour without overcooking. When you uncover the cooked rice, you will see steam holes in the surface.

RENDERING FAT FROM A DUCK

1. Remove the lumps of fat from the duck cavity, and discard them. (Also remove the neck skin and any fat in that area.) Cut off the wing tips and first joints.

2. Heat an iron skillet (or a wok) over high heat, and sprinkle a thin layer of salt (about 1 teaspoon) over the bottom of the pan. (I prefer coarse salt, but regular table salt will do.)

3. When both the pan and the salt are hot, place the duck in the pan, breast side down. The salt will draw the fat from the duck skin, and the duck will start to brown. Once this process starts, reduce the heat to medium high (or lower, if the fat starts to smoke).

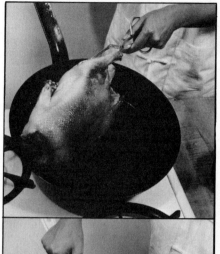

4. When the breast side is browned, turn the duck on its side with a pair of kitchen tongs, and brown as much of the side as possible. (The wing and leg joint will prevent some parts from being browned.) If the duck does not balance on its side by itself, use a pair of kitchen tongs to hold it in place. By tilting the duck back and forth and from side to side, you will be able to brown it fairly evenly. Be careful not to spill duck fat onto the stove; you do not want to start a grease fire.

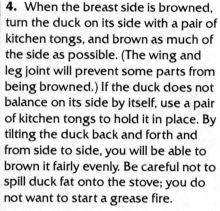

5. Turn off the flame, place a slotted spoon in the duck's cavity, and transfer the duck to the casserole breast side down (that is where the most meat is), first blotting off any excess fat with paper towels.

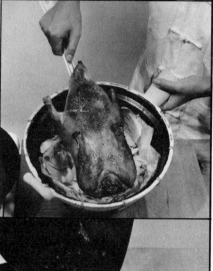

6. Pour off and discard the rendered duck fat.

CUTTING SPARERIBS INTO SMALL PIECES

1. With a medium-weight Chinese cleaver, chef's knife, or boning knife, trim off any extra fat on the back and front of the rack of spareribs.

2. Start to cut off the top section of the rack. (It has bone, cartilage, fat, and usable meat.) Find the spot where the long bones (the major part of the ribs) are attached to the top section.

3. Still using the Chinese cleaver (or other knife), separate the long bones. (You can use the heavy meat cleaver, but its weight makes it somewhat awkward.)

4. Place each rib, back side up, on the cutting surface. Switch to the heavy cleaver. Using a firm grip (the Chinese slicing grip, page 26, does not work), swing your forearm upward, and come down with the cleaver hard, aiming for the middle of the rib. Do not hold the rib in place with the other hand! (Let the pieces fly; you can rinse them off.) Concentrate on the spot you want to cut. (Think of being a Zen swordsman.)

5. If the bone is not cut through and is still wedged on the cleaver, swing down again. Thin bones are harder to cut through than thicker bones, which have much more marrow in them and are therefore somewhat spongy. If the bone is almost cut through, turn it over, and break it by snapping it with your thumb and fingers. Cut through the remaining meat with the cleaver.

6. Use the same technique to cut the top strip of meat into 2-inch pieces. The spareribs are now ready to be browned. Use the technique for rendering duck fat (page 30).

MAKING EGG - POUCH DUMPLINGS

1. Break the eggs into a mixing bowl, and beat them well with a regular fork.

2. Heat a small iron pan (a French crêpe pan is fine) over medium-high heat. When it is hot, add enough vegetable oil to coat the bottom of the pan. When the oil is hot, add about 2 tablespoons of egg to the pan. (Use a small ladle or gravy spoon.) Grasp the handle of the pan, and tilt and swirl the pan to spread the egg mixture so that it forms a small omelet.

3. Place about 1 heaping teaspoon of filling mixture in the center of the omelet. Use a spatula to fold the omelet into a pouch.

4. Do not let the omelet cook all the way through. The uncooked egg along the edges acts as a sealer for the dumpling.

5. Press the spatula around the outer rim of the dumpling to seal it. (By now, the handle of the pan will be hot, and you will have to hold it with a kitchen towel or potholder.)

6. As each dumpling is finished, transfer it to a lettuce-lined casserole (page 25), or an oiled plate. Continue to make the dumplings until the mixture is used up.

HACKING A CHICKEN

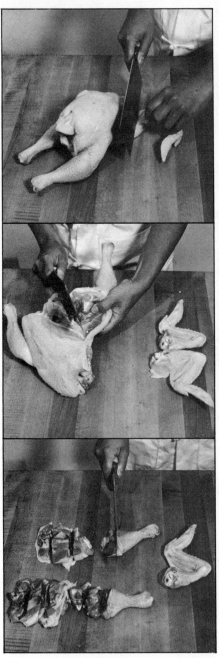

1. Place the chicken on the cutting surface, breast side down, wings toward you. Wiggle the wing up and down to see where it joins the body. With a firm slicing motion, cut through the skin and the connective tissue that holds the wing to the shoulder joint. Take off the other wing.

2. Place the chicken on its back with the ends of the drumsticks pointing toward you. Wiggle the thigh around to see where it is attached to the hip. Slice through the skin surrounding this joint. When the skin is cut through, you can see exactly where the thigh is attached to the body, and you can easily pop the joint out of its socket with a downward motion of the hand. With a slicing motion, cut through the meat and skin holding the thigh on.

3. Wiggle the thigh and drumstick to see where they are joined; slice through that joint. Chop the thigh and drumstick into 3 or 4 sections across the bone. Hold your elbow close to your body, and raise the cleaver 10 to 12 inches; snap your forearm and wrist down, making sharp contact with the chicken. If the pieces are not cut through cleanly, slice through the flesh still holding them together. Remove any splinters of bone. Repeat with the other leg.

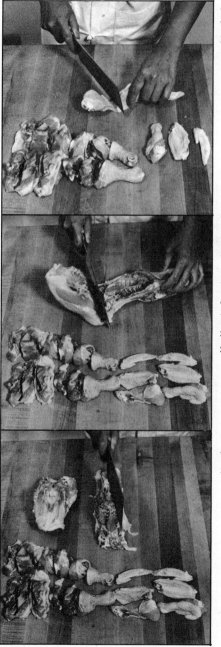

4. Wiggle the wing parts to see where they are joined to each other. Separate the pieces by slicing through the joints.

5. Hold the chicken by its back, neck end down. Look inside the cavity to see where the back ribs and breast ribs meet to form a V. Slice through the flesh and skin and through the apex of the V to the collarbone. Cut through the shoulder joint with a sharp whack. Separate the breast side from the back section.

6. Split the back in half lengthwise with a series of whacks along the spine.

7. Chop the lengths into 4 or 5 pieces.

8. Put the breast on the cutting surface skin side down. Split the breast in half lengthwise.

9. Now cut the breast halves into 4 or 5 pieces. You have now hacked a chicken. Congratulations.

INGREDIENTS

This chapter lists many ingredients that may seem esoteric or even forbidding. Although all or most of these ingredients are standard items in a Chinese home, I do not want the reader, to whom many of these supplies may not be readily familiar to feel that Chinese cooking is entirely out of the realm of possibility. Therefore, I have given a great deal of thought to the matter of suggesting alternative ingredients to people who do not live in a city with a Chinatown, and doing so without compromising on the quality of cooking and without turning the dish into a variation on chop suey. Many purists will insist that this cannot be done. I disagree. It is easy enough to cook with all the ingredients called for, but truly creative cooking comes in making do with what is available.

I have recently returned from a stay of more than six months in Israel, where I set up and cooked in a kosher Chinese restaurant at the Ramada Continental Hotel in Tel Aviv. The restrictions of the kosher dietary laws and the general unavailability of Chinese ingredients in Israel made this job the most challenging of my career; yet, I was still able to turn out very good Chinese food on a professional level. New Yorkers used to their choice of Chinese food in New York and French businessmen who prided themselves on having eaten in some of the finest restaurants all over the world asked to give their compliments to the chef personally — all this without Chinese black mushrooms, fresh ginger root, golden needles, cellophane noodles, cloud ears, hoisin sauce, or oyster sauce (which I personally feel to be a major Chinese condiment). I had to work with what was available: Israeli-produced soy sauce (not very good), a local sherry (good), kohlrabi (a good substitute for the crunchiness of bamboo shoots), and canned mushrooms instead of the dried. Ginger powder went into my marinades for meats, and I made a barbecue sauce using local catsup and an Israeli hot sauce. Canned water chestnuts were obtainable although even in New York I can live without them (a matter of personal taste.) I do admit that I traveled to Israel with ten pounds of salted black beans and three large cans of Japanese sesame oil, two ingredients I feel that I cannot do without to execute my style of cooking. Perhaps it will reassure you to know that many Chinese cooks do not use sesame oil to season food; don't think it is so terrible if you cannot get it. I feel that sesame oil provides an added dimension in taste and smell, but, again, that is a matter of personal taste.

Here are some general suggestions for substitutions (specific suggestions are given throughout the chapter): A brand of Japanese soy sauce that is now brewed in the United States and sold in supermarkets is quite acceptable in place of thin or black soy sauce. Star anise can sometimes be found in specialty food shops, but if you cannot find that, use aniseed. A dish made with substitutions will certainly not taste the same as it would if made with the called-for items. Nevertheless, the substitutions will give excellent flavor to the food. Experiment and adjust substitutions to suit yourself.

Many people associate bean sprouts with Chinese cooking, but you will not find them listed in this chapter because they should be used in stir-fried dishes, not in Chinese casserole cookery. More important, you will probably notice the absence of monosodium glutamate in the list. That is something about which I take a very strong personal stand. I do not use it, and I feel that it is not necessary for good Chinese cooking. Mediocre cooks use it as a crutch to intensify flavors; cooks who overuse it are no cooks at all. End of sermon.

BABY CORN

These miniature ears of corn are only 2 to 3 inches long and are canned in either water or brine. If you use the saltwater kind, rinse the corn under cold running water. If you do not use the entire can (and that is likely), put the remaining ears in a glass or plastic container, fill it with cold water, cover it, and store it in the refrigerator. Change the water daily, and use the corn within 5 days.

BAMBOO SHOOTS

These shoots arise from the sprouts or tips of bamboo plants and are canned in large pieces or sliced. Winter bamboo shoots are supposed to be the best tasting, but what you find on supermarket shelves are the summer shoots, which are of varying degrees of toughness or tenderness. Bamboo shoots are used not so much for their taste as for their texture. Restaurants rely on them as a filler in many stir-fried dishes. Store bamboo shoots, covered with water, in a glass or plastic container in the refrigerator; they will keep for a few weeks.

BEAN CURD

When mentioned without qualification, this means fresh bean curd (or bean cake), squares of custardlike pulp of soybeans about ½ inch thick by 3 inches square. Bean curd can be bought in Chinatowns, J-towns (Japanese towns), or in other parts of cities with a large enough Oriental population to support a bean curd factory. Chinese call it do fu; Japanese say tofu. There is a dried kind from Japan that is reconstituted in water; it resembles a sponge in both taste and texture and is not recommended. The Chinese make bean curd of a firm consistency; the Japanese prefer larger cakes of looser texture. I recommend the Chinese kind for the recipes in this book that require bean curd. Store bean curd, covered with cold water, in the refrigerator, and change the water daily. It will keep for several days but should be used up fairly quickly. It can be frozen, but when defrosted it has a very spongy texture. However, thawed bean curd can be used in long-simmered dishes.

BEAN CURD CHEESE, RED

This is bean curd that has been seasoned with red rice and salt and canned or put into jars. The can usually has a drawing of a square cake covered with a thick red sauce and is labeled Bean Cake. Transfer the contents to a jar, cap it, and store it in the refrigerator; it keeps indefinitely. This is a first cousin of white bean curd cheese; in Cantonese, it is called nom yee.

BEAN CURD CHEESE, WHITE

This is made by cutting cakes of fresh bean curd into four squares and putting them into a glass jar with a brine-alcohol solution. This cheese has a sharp, lovely taste that is not to everyone's liking. Often used as a condiment with congee or with rice in a very simple meal. Like red bean curd cheese, this is sometimes labeled just <u>bean curd</u>, although the white comes in jars and red usually in cans. The white also comes with a chili seasoning. (I use only the plain.) In Cantonese, this is called <u>foo yee</u>. Store white bean curd cheese on the shelf.

BEAN CURD, FRIED

Called <u>doe gawk</u> in Cantonese and <u>aga kiri</u> in Japanese, this is fresh bean curd that has been cubed and deep fried. <u>Doe gawk</u> resembles tiny, brown wrinkled pillows that seem almost hollow. This ingredient is not essential to the recipes that call for it, but it does give a nice color and texture to the dish. In Chinese markets, fried bean curd is sold loose or packed in plastic bags. Japanese stores sell it in plastic bags or canned. Store leftovers in the refrigerator, and use them within 1 week.

BEAN CURD SKIN, DRIED

This is made from dehydrated soybean milk and is usually sold in ½-pound packages. The skins measure about 1 ½ by 4 inches and are less than ⅛ inch thick. They look like thin pieces of light beige lacquered wood and are soaked in warm water until pliable (about ½ hour) before use. Bean curd skin, called <u>teem</u> <u>jook</u> in Cantonese, has a surprisingly meaty texture; it is good in vegetarian dishes and in combination with meats and vegetables. Store it in an airtight container on the shelf.

BEAN CURD STICKS

These sticks are made from soybean milk film that has been dried, rolled to ½-inch thickness, and bent into long pieces with a hairpin turn. These skins, called <u>foo</u> <u>jook</u> in Cantonese, are light beige in color and have a wrinkled, lacquered look. They come in ½-pound and 1-pound packages. Often used in soups or long-simmered dishes, they are soaked before using. Store bean curd sticks in an airtight container on the shelf.

BLACK BEANS, SALTED OR FERMENTED

These beans serve as a condiment. They have a very pungent odor that could scare away the timid, but do not be timid. They are almost always used in combination with garlic — a marriage made in heaven — and are delicious. The beans are interchangeably called fermented black beans and salted black beans. Restaurant menus refer to such dishes as Clams with Black Bean and Garlic Sauce, Lobster Cantonese, and Crab Cantonese. The beans come in ½-pound or 1-pound plastic bags or sometimes in a plastic bag sealed in a can. The beans should be rinsed before using. Store them in a capped jar on the shelf or in the refrigerator. If the beans dry out during storage, mix them with a little peanut oil before using them.

BROWN BEAN SAUCE, GROUND

This is a somewhat salty sauce, sometimes called bean paste, which comes in 1-pound cans. Some cookbooks list a brown bean sauce as well as a yellow bean sauce, which would lead the reader to think that they are different when they are actually the same. The confusion arises from the fact that in Chinese the word or character wong can be translated as either "brown" or "yellow," depending upon the whim of the translator. In Cantonese, this sauce is called meen see. This sauce also comes in a whole-bean form labeled simply bean sauce. (I once ran across a can of the ground bean sauce that the manufacturer had labeled grinding bean sauce.) Transfer any unused sauce to a glass jar, cap it, and refrigerate it; it will keep almost indefinitely.

CATSUP, TOMATO

The addition of a little bit of this condiment, originally non-Chinese, can make the difference between a mediocre curry and a very tasty Chinese one. It also is one of the ingredients of a good sweet-and-sour sauce and other dishes.

CELLOPHANE NOODLES

These are not noodles of the same type as egg noodles or spaghetti; they are made from a vegetable starch derived from mung beans and are known by many names: They are fun see in Cantonese (meaning "powdered silk"), saifon in Japanese. In Hawaii, they are long rice, and they may also be labeled — anywhere — bean threads. On menus, they may be called cellophane noodles or shiny noodles or transparent noodles. They come wrapped in cellophane packages weighing 2, 4, or 6 ounces and are inexpensive. Cellophane noodles are soaked in warm water before using. However, if they are to be used as a garnish for certain dishes, they are left dry, cut into short lengths and deep fried; they puff up instantaneously into a delicate, crisp tangle. Store cellophane noodles on the shelf in an airtight container. If cellophane noodles are unavailable, substitute thin egg noodles.

CHESTNUTS, DRIED

Shelled, peeled, and dried chestnuts from the Orient are sold by the pound, are reasonably priced, and save a lot of time and effort. They need to be soaked, refrigerated, for 24 hours, then simmered for 1 hour or so. These chestnuts have a mild smoky flavor and are very good in various mixed dishes as well as in stuffings. Store dried chestnuts in an airtight container at room temperature.

CHICKEN BROTH

Many of the recipes in this book call for a small amount of chicken broth. Use canned chicken broth that is light in flavor, not the double-strength kind, or make your own. (Avoid any of the powdered bases or cubes; they are much too salty.) If you use only a small amount out of the can, pour the rest into individual ice cube containers, and freeze them. When the cubes are frozen, you can pop them out of the containers and store them in a plastic bag in the freezer. If you have made a large amount of broth yourself, cool it and pour it into regular ice cube trays and freeze it.

CHILI OIL

This is a very hot liquid seasoning, red in color, made from vegetable oil and chili peppers. It is deceptive at first taste, so use it with considerable care. It comes in bottles; look for the bottle with a little drop spout, which easily regulates the amount of oil that comes out. Tabasco sauce is a good substitute.

CHILI PEPPERS, DRIED

Dried red chilies are available in whole or crushed form. The whole peppers are about 1½ inches long, although there is also a whole red pepper that is round and measures about ½ inch across. Both are equally potent. I break dried chili peppers in half and use both the skin and the seeds. For less hotness, you can omit the seeds. Italian red pepper flakes or crushed pepper flakes can be used as substitutes and are available in supermarkets.

CHILI POWDER

This powder is a combination of finely ground dried red chili peppers and other spices. Various brands are available at regular (i.e. American) grocery stores.

CHINESE PARSLEY (FRESH CORIANDER)

This is not parsley at all; it is fresh coriander, which is called cilantro in Hispanic stores. There are those who think it tastes like detergent! I happen to love it, but I realize it is an acquired taste. The leaves are a lighter green than Italian flat-leaved parsley, which fresh coriander somewhat resembles; they are usually sold by the bunch with the roots attached. To store the coriander, put it into a brown paper bag, put the bag inside a plastic bag, and refrigerate it. Powdered or whole coriander seeds are not a substitute for the fresh leaves; the flavor is completely different.

CHINESE SAUSAGE

If you have visited a Chinatown in the United States, you may have seen these sausages hanging in pairs on strings in the windows of grocery stores alongside whole roast ducks, soy sauce chickens, and Chinese bacon. There are two kinds of sausage: the sweet and the liver-flavored. Whenever sausage is called for in this book, the sweet variety is meant (the liver-flavored sausage is too strong). The sausages can be steamed over rice (just put them on top of the rice toward the end of cooking) for 15 minutes, then sliced and served as a side dish. They are also used with other meats and vegetables. A very good sausage is made in Vancouver; this kind is sold in ½- or 1-pound bags. It can be found in Chinatowns and in some West Coast supermarkets. The hanging sausages are sold by the pair according to weight. Store the sausage, wrapped in plastic, in the refrigerator or freezer; it will keep for several months.

CHUTNEY

This relish or condiment made of various fruits and seasonings is usually associated with Indian cooking. It comes bottled and is a standard supermarket item. Store chutney in the refrigerator once you have opened the bottle. It will keep for 2 or 3 months.

CLOUD EARS

These are one of two kinds of tree fungus used in Chinese cooking. (The other edible fungi, wood ears, are smaller in size.) Cloud ears are sold dried and look like flaky black ashes. Their small size will not prepare you for how large they become when they are soaked in warm water. (They must be soaked in water for at least ½ hour and rinsed well to free them of twigs and dirt.) "Cloud ears" is a literal translation from the Chinese. Cloud ears are sold by weight in bags and are sometimes labeled black fungus. Store them on the shelf in an airtight container.

CORNSTARCH

This is the thickening agent used in most Chinese cooking in the United States; it does a good job and is inexpensive. If you mix the thickening for a sauce ahead of time, be sure to stir the cornstarch and water binder at the last minute because the starch sinks to the bottom of the cup or bowl it was mixed in if it is left standing. Different brands of cornstarch have different degrees of strength. Strength also varies with the degree of freshness. Thus, the same measure of cornstarch will not always produce the same amount of thickening. Keep a sharp eye on the sauce, and use your good judgment about adding more or less cornstarch.

CURRY POWDER

Curry is a combination of several dried spices, from five to fifty, ground to a powder. The curry powders sold in American supermarkets are satisfactory, or you may want to use an Indian brand.

DUCK EGGS, SALTED

Fresh duck eggs put into brine for 5 to 6 weeks end up as salted duck eggs; this is a way to prevent eggs from going to waste. In home-style cooking, the salted duck egg is hard-cooked, peeled, quartered, and served as an accompaniment to white rice or congee (jook). They are purchased loose and are best stored in the refrigerator.

FIVE-SPICE POWDER

This brownish-red powder is a blend of star anise, cloves, fennel, Szechuan peppercorns (flower pepper), and cinnamon. It is used sparingly in a number of dishes. Star anise can be used alone as a substitute for five-spice powder.

GARLIC

Only fresh garlic is called for in this book. Use garlic powder or garlic salt only if fresh garlic is not available. (Is that possible in this day and age?) To peel garlic easily, cut off the stem end, then give the clove a gentle whack with the flat side of a cleaver or chef's knife. The skin will slip off easily.

GINGER ROOT, FRESH

The root of the tropical ginger plant is very spicy. Besides contributing flavor to many dishes, it is used to neutralize fishy or gamy tastes, so it is sometimes referred to as a defisher. Biting directly into a piece of ginger root can be unpleasant. Yet, when used correctly, ginger imparts a subtle fragrance to food. Many of the meat marinades in this book call for freshly grated ginger root. The Japanese have a little kitchen tool ordinarily used to grate daikon (Japanese radish or Chinese turnip) that is ideal for grating ginger root very fine. A nutmeg grater will work almost as well. However, the finest section of a four-sided grater usually clogs up too quickly. The alternative to grating ginger is to slice off a section about ⅛ inch thick, and mash it with the broad side of a cleaver or chef's knife. Mashing the slice crushes the fibers and releases more flavor; the slice of ginger should be removed before the food is served.

If you must use powdered ginger, ½ teaspoon equals a ⅛-inch slice. In a pinch, I have even used finely minced candied ginger. The best way to store fresh ginger is to put the root into a small brown paper bag and then into a plastic bag. Close the bags, keep the ginger in the vegetable compartment of the refrigerator. (If the ginger root is wrapped directly in plastic, it will sweat and grow mold.) Ginger is sold by weight.

GOLDEN NEEDLES

These are dried tiger lily buds and are often called <u>dried lily flower</u> or <u>tiger lily</u> <u>stems</u>. (Of course, they are not stems.) Processors, in labeling their packages, often confuse matters even more by calling them <u>dried vegetable</u>. I prefer to call them by the literal translation of their Cantonese name, <u>gum jum</u>: "golden needle." Golden needles are used in vegetarian dishes, in combination meat and vegetable dishes, and in soups. They are soaked in water before using. If the base of a bud seems especially hard, nip it off. Golden needles can be knotted in the middle for a decorative, amusing effect. They are sold by weight. Store golden needles in an airtight container at room temperature.

HAM

Some recipes in this book call for a small amount of ham. The packaged sandwich ham found in supermarkets is fine, although I prefer the smoked ham that is also found in the sandwich meat section.

HOISIN SAUCE

This is a sweetish, thick, dark purplish-brown sauce that comes in 1-pound and 5-pound cans. Restaurants usually serve it with Peking duck; it is sometimes erroneously called plum sauce, which is really a Chinese chutney. Transfer the sauce to a glass jar, cap it, and store it in the refrigerator. Hoisin sauce keeps for a long time.

HORSERADISH, BOTTLED

This is the grated root of a plant that has a very sharp flavor. It usually comes in 4-ounce bottles and is readily available in supermarkets, usually in the refrigerated dairy section. Store horseradish in the refrigerator; it will keep for 2 or 3 months.

LICHEE FRUIT

Lichees grow on small trees and are indigenous to southern China. A wonderful tea is made from the leaves, but it is the fruit, in season for a very short period at the beginning of summer, that is considered a great delicacy. The recipes in this book call for canned lichees. The fresh fruit, roughly 1 inch in diameter, has a brown outer shell that peels off to reveal a whitish meat which has the texture of a peeled grape; it has a brown pit. The canned fruit has found its way to supermarkets. Dried lichee fruit has a hollow shell which , when broken, reveals a wrinkled brown fruit. It has something of the taste and texture of a raisin. Once opened, canned lichee fruits should be transferred to a covered glass or plastic container and stored in the refrigerator. They will keep (in their own syrup) for up to 1 week.

MUSHROOMS, DRIED BLACK

These dried black mushrooms come from the Orient, are sold by weight, and are very expensive. Fortunately, a few go a long way. They must be soaked before using. Trim off and discard the stems, but save the mushroom liquid for stock or sauce. Store dried mushrooms at room temperature in an airtight container.

MUSHROOMS, STRAW

These mushrooms resemble the French <u>champignons</u> and usually come in cans. They have a nice texture and a nice taste. Any leftovers can be stored in a jar in the refrigerator for a few days.

MUSTARD, DIJON-STYLE

This condiment is sold in paste form. The best-known variety comes from Dijon, the capital of the province of Burgundy, France. It comes in jars and is available in supermarkets. Store the mustard in the refrigerator.

OYSTER SAUCE

This essential item in Cantonese kitchens is usually labeled <u>oyster-flavored sauce</u>, which seems to imply that the sauce is artificially flavored. It is, in fact, a sauce made from oysters; and it has a rich, full-bodied, unique flavor. This sauce is very good as a separate condiment for boiled chicken or leftover roast meat. It comes in bottles, and for those who use a lot of it, there is a 5-pound can. If you buy the can, decant the sauce into bottles, cap them, and store them at room temperature.

PEPPER, WHITE

Many recipes in this book call for white pepper; you may wonder what the difference between white and black pepper is. A white peppercorn is a black peppercorn with the outer layer removed. It has a more subtle and delicate taste, yet it can add fire to a dish. It is sold both whole and ground. White pepper tastes best when ground fresh in a pepper mill. Store it on the shelf.

PLUM SAUCE

This condiment made of plums, other fruits, and seasonings is really a Chinese chutney. It usually comes in 1-pound cans. Once plum sauce has been opened, it should be transferred to glass jars or plastic containers and refrigerated. It will keep for 2 or 3 months.

RICE

The kind of rice the Chinese eat is a long-grain rice. Different types of rice absorb different amounts of water, and all the instructions in this book are for the long-grain variety. Most supermarkets carry their own brand, which is sometimes labeled extra fancy long-grain rice. Use it, but disregard the instructions telling you not to wash the rice; Chinese wash rice until the water is crystal clear to take out the extra starch and to prevent the cooked rice from being gummy.

SALT

This substance, used as a condiment or as a preservative, has a very ancient history. It was often used as payment (salarium is the Latin source of the word salary). The recipes in this book do not call for the use of salt as a seasoning (soy sauce is used instead). Rather, salt is used as a cooking medium (as in Salt-cooked Chicken and Piquant Salt-baked Cornish Hens), to brown spareribs, and as part of a technique to render duck fat (see page 30). I prefer the coarse or kosher salt to the free-flowing small-grained salt for aesthetic reasons, or possibly as a minor food snobbism among " serious" cooks. If coarse salt is unavailable, use the regular, by all means.

SESAME OIL

This dark, highly aromatic oil made from toasted sesame seeds is one of the great contributions the Orient has made to mankind. It is quite different from the kind of sesame oil sold in health food stores, which is clear, bland, and expensive. Sesame oil is used as a perfume, and is a basic part of Chinese cookery, even though many Chinese restaurants do not use it. Use sesame oil with discretion. A little can make the difference between a mediocre dish and a very good one, but too much can overwhelm the taste buds. Sesame oil comes in bottles of various sizes; larger amounts come in cans. For some reason, Japanese brands are more readily available in large quantities than Chinese brands. Store it on the shelf.

SHERRY

When sherry is called for in this book, I mean California sherry (straight or medium, depending upon how the winery labels it). A smaller amount of gin or vodka is a good substitute if there is no domestic sherry in the house. Please save imported sherries for cocktail time, not for cooking. Store sherry, tightly capped, at room temperature.

SNOW PEAS

This is a Chinese pea that is listed in seed catalogs as Peas: Chinese edible pod (sugar peas); the French call it mange pois tout. This vegetable gives wonderful taste, texture, and color to a dish. In the recipes calling for snow peas, I specify that they should be added to the casserole during the last 5 minutes of cooking so that their texture will be retained. If fresh snow peas are not available, do not use the frozen kind. Instead, substitute green beans, broccoli, or some other green vegetable.

SOY SAUCE

This major ingredient in Chinese cooking is made by fermenting a mixture of cooked soybeans, wheat flour, yeast, salt, and water and then aging the mixture, which was traditionally exposed to sunlight in stone crocks. The soy sauce made in the United States is aged chemically. Some brands of Oriental soy sauce are available on the shelves of supermarkets. Ask the manager of the store to stock the larger-sized bottles (for convenience and economy). Soy sauce can be stored on the shelf. There follow two kinds of soy sauce used in this book, but if neither is available, use the Japanese soy sauce that is carried in most supermarkets.

Thin (or light) soy sauce: a light grade of soy sauce, delicate in flavor, often used at the table for dipping, especially in Cantonese dumpling houses. Thin soy sauce appears on most of the bottle labels found in Chinatowns in the United States; the names thin and light are interchangeable.

Black (or dark) soy sauce: a heavier, darker, and saltier soy sauce. Most labels read black soy sauce. To confuse the nomenclature even more, there is something sold as soy molasses or thick soy, which is used in some Chinese restaurants to give a dark color to fried rice; this kind is not called for in this book. Black soy sauce is preferable to the thin sauce for red-cooked dishes because it gives a dark color to the cooked food.

STAR ANISE

This dried, eight-pointed spice with a licorice flavor is used in red-cooked dishes. Star anise is sold by weight. Store it at room temperature in an airtight jar. If you have to substitute, use 2 tablespoons anise seed for 2 whole star anise.

SUGAR

Unless otherwise specified, the sugar called for in this book is granulated white sugar. Please understand that the purpose of sugar is not to make the dish sweet. Rather, a small amount of sugar in a dish pulls the various flavors into a cohesive whole. Occasionally, brown sugar or rock sugar is used in Chinese cooking to give a dish more body or a lustrous glaze.

TANGERINE PEEL, DRIED

Available in Chinese stores and sold either by the piece or by weight. You can make your own by peeling a tangerine, scraping most of the white pith from the peel, and letting the peel dry in the air for a few days. Or place the peel on the part of a gas stove directly over the pilot light; the peel should dry out overnight. Store the dried peel in an airtight jar at room temperature.

THOUSAND-YEAR-OLD EGGS

This is a somewhat fanciful term for duck eggs preserved in a mixture of lime, mud, and used tea leaves. During the curing process, the egg yolk turns a greenish-black color and the egg white a dark amber. The texture is a cross between a hard-cooked egg and a thick aspic. The egg has the taste of a hard-cooked egg, so do not let the color of the egg put you off. The egg is often served as an hors d'oeuvre or an accompaniment to congee. To prepare, carefully crack or scrape off the caked mud on the egg, rinse the shell of any remaining coating, then crack and peel it as you would a hard-cooked egg. Cut the egg into quarters (some do this by using a strong thread to make a clean cut), and serve it with slices of red or pickled ginger or pickled scallions.

VEGETABLE OIL FOR COOKING

Peanut oil is the oil of choice for the recipes in this book. Butter and olive oil are not suitable, but soy, corn, cottonseed, or safflower oil may be used in place of peanut oil.

VEGETARIAN STEAK

I have heard of a restaurant in Hong Kong that the locals like to take tourists to. An array of food is served, and the host will ask, "How did you like the duck? How did you like the chicken? How did you like the ham?" When the guest responds to these questions, he or she is then told that all the dishes were made of vegetable products and that they were dining in a vegetarian restaurant where the cooks are exceptionally skilled in preparing soybean and gluten products that take on the texture and taste of various meats.

Vegetarian steak from the

Far East comes in cans already cooked and seasoned, and can be eaten cold or reheated. I prefer to incorporate this meat substitute with other ingredients, as I do in Buddha's Delight Vegetarian Casserole, a dish often served on Chinese New Year's Eve.

Many Chinese companies ship food to the United States, and the labels and names for this meat substitute differ from company to company, which can confuse the shopper. I use the kind that is labeled Chai Pow Yu (braised gluten), which translates as "mock abalone" or "vegetarian abalone." You might try health food stores, which carry an American vegetarian steak. Gluten is flour mixed with water and kneaded under water to work out much of the starch. The Chinese usually fry pieces of this gluten, then stew it with soy sauce and various spices.

VINEGAR

When it comes to vinegar, I prefer using rice vinegar, which is made in Japan and can be found on the shelves of many supermarkets. This vinegar is light and delicate and delicious for salad dressings. Use white vinegar if rice vinegar is not available. For sweet-and-sour sauce, I prefer cider vinegar.

WATER CHESTNUTS

The Chinese name for water chestnuts translates as horses hooves, which they in fact resemble — another example of the poetic descriptiveness of Chinese names for foods. These walnut-sized bulbs come peeled and water-packed in cans. They don't have much taste, but they have a nice, crunchy texture. Fresh water chestnuts can be found in Chinatowns. They have a tough brown outer skin and are a little tedious to peel and trim, but they have a wonderful, sweet taste. The first time I ever saw a fresh water chestnut was when I was a small child and was visiting my father's restaurant (I loved going there because I could get "free" ice cream). I would watch the waiters doing something I found quite fascinating: They sat around peeling small, dark things with Chinese cleavers.

Put leftover canned water chestnuts in a glass jar filled with water, and store it in the refrigerator, changing the water every 2 to 3 days. If the water is changed often, the water chestnuts will keep for at least 1 or 2 weeks. Fresh water chestnuts will keep for about 2 weeks in the refrigerator if you put them into a brown paper bag and then into a plastic one.

WOOD EARS

This dried black fungus is thicker than its relative, the cloud ear or cloud fungus. They are sometimes referred to as tree mushrooms, tree ears, or black fungus. Wood ears are soaked in warm water before using, then well rinsed. They are sold by weight in plastic bags. Store wood ears in an airtight container on the shelf.

BEEF

Traditionally, beef has not been much used by the Chinese because China was, and still is, an agrarian nation. The land is used primarily for raising crops rather than for rearing cattle. The ox that pulled the plow was such a useful animal that the government, from time to time, actually prohibited its slaughter. Therefore, because beef was forbidden, it became a highly prized meat to eat, although the meat of an animal that had spent its whole life at hard labor could not have been otherwise than tough and stringy. In contrast, the Chinese in the United States have made great use of beef because it is in great supply. Most of the cuts of beef used in the recipes in this chapter, such as short ribs, oxtails, and organ meats, are economy cuts that are made tender by long cooking.

RED-COOKED POT ROAST WITH VEGETABLES

Whenever I give a large cast party, I like to serve this dish. I make it the day before, refrigerate it overnight, take it out before I go to the theater, then reheat it when I come home with the cast and crew. By the time they have had hors d'oeuvres and drinks, the pot roast has been reheated and sliced and is ready to be served.

Figure on about one-half pound of meat (the weight when you buy the meat) for a generous portion. You can always stretch the dish by adding more vegetables and including potatoes.

Ingredients

Vegetable oil for browning meat and onions
4- to 5-pound boneless beef chuck roast
2 large onions, cut in half from top to bottom, peeled, and cut into ¼-inch slices along the grain

Braising Liquid

½ cup black soy sauce
1 cup sherry
1 teaspoon sugar
4 cloves garlic, peeled and flattened
3 whole star anise
½ teaspoon white pepper
1-pound can peeled tomatoes, including packing liquid

Other Vegetables

4 carrots, peeled and cut into 1-inch diagonal chunks
4 ribs celery, cut into 1-inch diagonal slices

Binder and Final Seasoning

2   tablespoons cornstarch
2   tablespoons cold water
½   teaspoon sesame oil

Instructions

1. Put a large, heavy skillet or a wok over high heat, and pour in
    1½ tablespoons of oil, or enough to film the cooking
    surface; tilt the pan to cover the cooking surface thoroughly.
    When the oil is very hot, put the chuck roast into the pan,
    and brown it on all sides. Transfer the meat to a 3½- or
    4-quart casserole.

2. Add the onions to the fat in the pan, and cook them,
    stirring, until they are translucent. Drain excess oil from the
    pan.

3. Add the braising liquid ingredients to the onions, and bring
    everything to a boil. Pour the hot mixture over the meat in
    the casserole.

4. Add enough water to barely cover the meat. Bring the
    liquid to a boil, lower the heat, cover the casserole, and
    simmer the meat gently for 1½ hours, turning it
    occasionally.

5. Add the carrots and celery, and simmer the pot roast,
    covered, for 1 hour, again turning the meat from time to
    time. Uncover the casserole, and simmer for about ½ hour
    longer to reduce the liquid.

6. Mix the cornstarch and water, stir the binder into the
    simmering sauce, and cook the sauce briefly (2 to 4
    minutes) until slightly thickened.

7. Stir in the sesame oil as the final seasoning, and serve the
    pot roast hot.

Preparation time: 10 minutes
Cooking time: 3 hours
Serves: 8

MINCED BEEF WITH CELLOPHANE NOODLES AND VEGETABLES

This is an inexpensive dish and a good meat stretcher. For a nice summertime variation, drain off any surplus juice, and serve the hot beef and vegetables accompanied by a platter of crisp lettuce leaves. At the table, spoon some of the mixture into the center of a lettuce leaf, and roll the leaf like a tortilla. The coolness and crunchiness of the lettuce contrast beautifully with the heat and texture of the filling.

Marinade

4	teaspoons thin soy sauce
4	teaspoons sherry
½	teaspoon sugar
¼	teaspoon sesame oil

Other Ingredients

1	pound ground chuck
4	dried black Oriental mushrooms
½	cup water chestnuts, cut into ¼-inch dice
½	cup bamboo shoots, rinsed and cut into ¼-inch dice
1	cup frozen peas, thawed
	2-ounce package cellophane noodles, soaked in warm water for 30 minutes, drained, and cut into 2-inch lengths
	Vegetable oil for browning beef

Braising Liquid

2	tablespoons thin soy sauce
2	tablespoons sherry
1	tablespoon oyster sauce
½	teaspoon sugar

1   cup reserved mushroom-soaking liquid (see step 2)
½   cup chicken broth (if needed; see step 5)

Final Seasoning

½   teaspoon sesame oil

Instructions

1. Mix the marinade ingredients until the sugar dissolves. Add the marinade to the ground beef, and mix well. Let the mixture rest at room temperature for 1 hour.

2. Cover the mushrooms with warm water, and soak them for 1 hour. Drain the mushrooms, reserving the soaking liquid. Cut off and discard stems, and cut the caps into quarters.

3. Mix the braising liquid ingredients in a 2-quart casserole. Finish preparing the mushrooms, water chestnuts, bamboo shoots, peas, and cellophane noodles.

4. Put a large frying pan or a wok over high heat, and add enough vegetable oil to coat the pan (about 1½ tablespoons), tilting the pan to cover the cooking surface. When the oil is hot, add the marinated beef, mushrooms, water chestnuts, bamboo shoots, peas, and cellophane noodles. Fry them over medium-high heat for 5 minutes, tossing the ingredients often. Transfer everything to the casserole containing the braising liquid.

5. Bring the liquid in the casserole to a boil over high heat. Reduce the heat to medium low, cover the casserole, and simmer the ingredients gently for 25 minutes, checking from time to time. If the cellophane noodles absorb all the liquid, add enough chicken broth to prevent sticking.

6. Drizzle the sesame oil into the casserole, and stir the ingredients well. Serve the beef hot.

Preparation time: 1 hour to marinate and soak mushrooms
Cooking time: ½ hour
Serves: 4

BEEF CHUNKS IN BLACK BEAN, GARLIC, AND EGG SAUCE

A beef stew is a beef stew is a beef stew — but not when you use Chinese salted black beans and garlic. The egg is added to the sauce for texture and looks.

Ingredients

Vegetable oil for browning meat and onions

2 pounds beef stew meat, cut into 1-inch cubes
1 large onion, cut in half from top to bottom, peeled, and cut into ¼-inch slices along the grain
3 tablespoons salted black beans, rinsed in water, drained, and mashed
4 cloves garlic, peeled and finely minced
4 carrots, peeled and cut into ½-inch diagonal chunks
3 ribs celery, cut into ½-inch diagonal pieces
2 medium-sized potatoes, peeled and cut into 1-inch cubes
6 water chestnuts, cut into ⅛-inch slices
1 cup frozen peas, thawed

Braising Liquid

¼ cup black soy sauce
¼ cup sherry
½ teaspoon sugar
1 slice fresh ginger root, ⅛-inch thick, flattened
1 cup chicken broth

Binder and Final Seasoning

4 teaspoons cornstarch
4 teaspoons cold water
2 eggs
½ teaspoon sesame oil

Instructions

1. Heat a large skillet or a wok, and pour in enough vegetable oil to film the pan (about 1½ tablespoons), tilting the pan to coat the cooking surface thoroughly. When the oil is hot, add the beef and onions, and brown them, stirring, over high heat.

2. Add the mashed black beans and minced garlic, and mix them well with the meat and onions. Remove the skillet from the heat.

3. Mix the braising liquid ingredients in a 3½-quart (or larger) casserole. Add the meat and onions to the pot, along with the black beans, carrots, celery, and potatoes. Stir everything.

4. Bring the liquid to a boil over high heat. Reduce the heat to medium low, cover the casserole, and simmer the stew for about 1¾ hours, or until the meat is almost done.

5. Add the water chestnuts and peas, and simmer for another 15 minutes. Remove the slice of ginger.

6. Mix the cornstarch and water binder, and stir it into the sauce. Break the eggs into the sauce, and stir. Simmer the stew another 5 minutes.

7. Drizzle the sesame oil over the stew, and give all the ingredients a final stir. Serve the stew hot.

Preparation time: 15 minutes
Cooking time: 2 hours
Serves: 8

SPICY BEEF AND BEAN CURD CASSEROLE

Because bean curd is a rather bland-tasting food, it provides a pleasant surprise in spicy dishes. In this recipe, the bean curd's blandness and what I call its cool quality make a nice contrast with the hotness of the chili peppers.

Ingredients

Vegetable oil for browning beef and onions
2 pounds beef stew meat, cut into 1-inch cubes
1 large onion, cut in half from top to bottom, peeled, and cut into ¼-inch slices along the grain

Braising Liquid

2 tablespoons thin soy sauce
2 tablespoons sherry
¼ teaspoon sugar
2 cloves garlic, peeled and flattened
1 slice fresh ginger root, ⅛-inch thick, flattened
2 dried chili peppers, broken in half (use both seeds and pods)
2 tablespoons hoisin sauce
1 tablespoon ground brown bean sauce
2 tablespoons vinegar (either cider or distilled white)
½ cup chicken broth

Other Ingredients

2 squares bean curd, cut into 1-inch cubes
2 sweet green peppers, stemmed, seeded, deribbed, and cut into 1-inch squares

Binder and Final Seasoning

2 teaspoons cornstarch
2 teaspoons cold water
½ teaspoon sesame oil

Instructions

1. Put a large frying pan or a wok over high heat, and add enough oil (about 1½ tablespoons), to film the pan, tilting the pan to coat the entire cooking surface. When the oil is hot, add the beef and onions, and brown them, turning the pieces often.

2. Mix the braising liquid in a 3-quart casserole. Add the beef and onions to the casserole. Bring the liquid to a boil over high heat. Reduce the heat to medium low, cover the casserole, and simmer the meat for 1 hour.

3. Add the cubes of bean curd and squares of green pepper to the casserole, and simmer the stew for another ½ hour. Discard the slice of ginger.

4. Mix the cornstarch and water binder. Stir the binder into the stew, and cook for a few minutes, stirring occasionally, until the sauce is slightly thickened.

5. Add the sesame oil, give a final stir, and serve the casserole hot.

Preparation time: 10 to 15 minutes
Cooking time: 1½ hours
Serves: 4 or 5

DEVILED SHORT RIBS

Short ribs are not my favorite cut of meat: The bones weigh so much, and the meat can be tough and dry. But it seemed imperative to include a recipe for them. Although I grumbled all the way home from the market, I was very satisfied with the results. I think you'll like these pungently seasoned ribs.

Ingredients

Salt for browning short ribs
4   pounds meaty beef short ribs, trimmed of surplus fat, separated, and cut into 2-inch pieces

Braising Liquid

1   cup black soy sauce
1   cup sherry
1   teaspoon sugar
4   cloves garlic, peeled and flattened
1   slice fresh ginger root, ¼-inch thick, flattened
2   whole star anise
2   dried chili peppers, broken in half (use both seeds and pods)
½   cup water

Vegetables

1   large onion, cut in half from top to bottom, peeled, and cut into ¼-inch slices along the grain
6   carrots, peeled and cut into 1-inch diagonal chunks
3   ribs celery, cut into 1-inch diagonal pieces

Binder and Final Seasonings

1   tablespoon cornstarch
1   tablespoon cold water
½   teaspoon sesame oil
2   tablespoons Dijon-style mustard

Instructions

1. Set a large frying pan or a wok over high heat, and sprinkle about 1 teaspoon of salt into it. When the salt is hot, add half the short ribs, and brown them on all sides (about 8 minutes).

2. Meanwhile, mix the braising liquid ingredients in a 4-quart casserole.

3. With a slotted spoon, transfer the browned short ribs to the casserole, draining them of excess fat. Brown the remaining short ribs in the same fat, and transfer them to the casserole. Turn the ribs in the braising liquid to coat them well.

4. Bring the liquid to a boil over high heat. Reduce the heat to medium low, cover the casserole, and simmer the short ribs for about 2½ hours, turning them from time to time.

5. Add the onion, carrots, and celery, and mix them in well. Simmer the meat and vegetables for 1 hour. Remove the piece of ginger.

6. Mix the cornstarch and water binder, and add it to the braising liquid.

7. Remove about 1 cup of sauce from the casserole, and stir the sesame oil and Dijon-style mustard into it. Pour this mixture back into the pot, and mix everything well. Cook, stirring, for a few minutes, until the sauce has thickened lightly. Serve the short ribs hot.

Preparation time: 10 minutes
Cooking time: 4 hours
Serves: 4 to 6

STUFFED GREEN PEPPERS IN CURRY SAUCE

Stuffed peppers seem to be an American favorite, and Chinese kitchens produce many foods involving stuffings. Here is how a Chinese chef might combine ingredients from two cuisines — or three if you count the curry flavoring, originally Indian but well established in China.

Ingredients

4 sweet green (bell) peppers

Filling

1½ pounds ground beef
6 water chestnuts, diced fine (⅛-inch cubes)
½ cup cooked rice
1 egg, lightly beaten
4 teaspoons thin soy sauce
4 teaspoons sherry
1 teaspoon sugar
½ teaspoon sesame oil
⅛ teaspoon grated fresh ginger root
¼ teaspoon white pepper
2 teaspoons cornstarch mixed with 2 teaspoons cold water

Braising Liquid

¼ cup thin soy sauce
¼ cup sherry
1 teaspoon sugar
2 tablespoons curry powder (or to taste)
½ teaspoon chili powder
1 tablespoon tomato catsup
½ cup chicken broth

Binder and Final Seasoning

2 teaspoons cornstarch
2 teaspoons cold water
½ teaspoon sesame oil

Instructions

1. Cut the peppers in half horizontally, and remove the seeds and the white parts of the ribs.

2. In a large mixing bowl, blend all the filling ingredients. (To make sure the filling is really well mixed, use your hands.)

3. Stuff the mixture into the pepper halves.

4. Mix the braising liquid in a 10- or 11-inch casserole. Set the peppers in the liquid, with the stuffing facing up.

5. Bring the liquid to a boil over high heat. Reduce the heat to medium low, cover the pan, and simmer the peppers for 1 hour, or until the shells and the filling are done.

6. Mix the cornstarch and water binder, and stir it gently into the braising liquid around the peppers. Simmer the sauce for a few minutes, stirring it carefully so that the peppers are not damaged, until it has thickened a little.

7. Stir the sesame oil into the sauce, and serve the peppers hot in the casserole.

Preparation time: 15 minutes
Cooking time: 1 hour
Serves: 4

STUFFED CABBAGE ROLLS

Cabbage rolls seem to be like stuffed green peppers: Versions of both appear in many cuisines. These dishes, like fried rice, are a good way to use little odds and ends of leftovers. Although this recipe calls for ground beef, there is no reason why you can't substitute leftover pot roast, poultry, or any other kind of meat.

Ingredients

10 large cabbage leaves

Stuffing

1½ pounds ground beef
6 water chestnuts, diced fine (⅛-inch cubes)
½ cup cooked rice
3 tablespoons minced ham
1 egg, lightly beaten
4 teaspoons thin soy sauce
4 teaspoons sherry
1 teaspoon sugar
½ teaspoon sesame oil
⅛ teaspoon grated fresh ginger root
¼ teaspoon white pepper

Braising Liquid

¼ cup thin soy sauce
¼ cup sherry
½ teaspoon sugar
1 whole star anise
  8-ounce can tomato sauce

Binder and Final Seasoning

1 teaspoon cornstarch
1 teaspoon cold water
½ teaspoon sesame oil

Instructions

1. Blanch the cabbage leaves for 5 minutes in a large pot of boiling water; then cool them under running cold water, and drain them well.

2. Combine the stuffing ingredients in a large bowl, and mix them until everything is well blended.

3. Divide the stuffing into 10 portions. Put a portion at the base of each cabbage leaf, and roll the leaf up envelope fashion, tucking in the sides midway to keep the filling in place.

4. Mix the braising liquid in a 10- or 11-inch shallow casserole, and lay the cabbage rolls in the sauce, seams down.

5. Bring the liquid to a boil over high heat. Reduce the heat to medium low, cover the pan, and simmer the rolls for 30 minutes. Turn the cabbage rolls over, and simmer them for another 30 minutes.

6. Lift the cabbage rolls onto a platter with a slotted spoon, and keep them warm.

7. Mix the cornstarch and water binder, and stir it into the liquid. Simmer the sauce for a few minutes, stirring gently, until it thickens slightly.

8. Add the sesame oil, and give a final stir. Pour the sauce over the cabbage rolls, and serve them hot.

Preparation time: 20 minutes
Cooking time: 1 hour
Serves: 5

RED-COOKED OXTAIL STEW

Although oxtails are readily available in supermarkets and are usually an economical buy, a surprising number of people are unacquainted with this variety meat. The cartilage between the joints in the tail gives a wonderfully rich, tacky texture to oxtail stew. Oxtails take a long time to cook. Of course, the time will vary, depending upon the size and age of the animal, but count on at least three hours. Oxtails taste even better rewarmed and served the next day.

Red cooking is a term the Chinese use for stewing dishes in liquid including black soy sauce and, often, star anise. Supposedly, the soy sauce gives these dishes a red color, but they certainly look dark brown to me.

Ingredients

Salt for browning oxtails and onions
3½ pounds oxtails, disjointed and trimmed of surplus fat
1   large onion, cut in half from top to bottom, peeled, and cut into ¼-inch slices along the grain

Braising Liquid

½   cup black soy sauce
¾   cup sherry
1   teaspoon sugar
2   whole star anise
3   cloves garlic, peeled and flattened
1-pound can peeled tomatoes, including packing liquid

Other Vegetables

3   carrots, peeled and cut into ½-inch diagonal slices
3   ribs celery, cut into ½-inch diagonal slices
1   cup frozen peas, thawed

Binder and Final Seasoning

1   tablespoon cornstarch
1   tablespoon cold water
½   teaspoon sesame oil

Instructions

1. Put a large, heavy skillet or a wok over high heat, and sprinkle about 1 teaspoon of salt over the bottom. When the salt is hot, add the oxtails, and brown them on all sides. (They will render enough of their own fat for this browning to take place.) Add the onions to the pan shortly after the oxtails, and brown them together.

2. Combine the braising liquid ingredients in a 4-quart casserole. Transfer the oxtails and onions to the casserole, using a slotted spoon to drain the fat. Mix everything well, and bring the liquid to a boil over high heat. Reduce the heat to medium low, cover the casserole, and simmer the oxtails gently for 3 hours, or until the meat is tender.

3. Add the carrots and celery, and simmer the stew for 40 minutes. Add the peas, and simmer for 20 minutes longer.

4. Skim all possible fat from the stew. Stir the cornstarch and water binder together, and mix it into the stew. Cook over medium heat for a few minutes, stirring occasionally, until the sauce thickens lightly.

5. Stir in the sesame oil, and serve hot.

Preparation time: 15 to 20 minutes
Cooking time: About 4 hours
Serves: 4

HUNAM OXTAIL STEW

Defining regional cuisines is an elusive task. One can describe the general characteristics of the cooking in some areas, but it is not as if each province were hermetically sealed and isolated. Cooking, like ideas, travels, and there is so much intermingling of tastes and techniques that a precise definition of separate regional cuisines becomes impossible. This recipe uses chili peppers liberally, one characteristic of Hunam (and Szechuan) cooking, but frankly, I'm not sure what makes it Hunam. I have spoken to many food writers, restaurant people, cooks, and cooking instructors and come away with the same vague impression: It's close to Szechuan, it's hot, and it's Hunam because that's what we call it!

Ingredients

Salt for browning oxtails and onions
3½ pounds oxtails, disjointed and trimmed of surplus fat

Braising Liquid

½   cup black soy sauce
¾   cup sherry
1   teaspoon sugar
3   cloves garlic, peeled and flattened
4   dried chili peppers, broken in half (use both seeds and pods)
2   whole star anise
¾   cup water

Onions

2   large onions, cut in half from top to bottom, peeled, and cut into ¼-inch slices along the grain

Binder and Final Seasoning

1   teaspoon cornstarch
1   teaspoon cold water
½   teaspoon sesame oil

Instructions

1. Heat a large, heavy skillet or a wok over a high flame. Scatter about 1 teaspoon of salt over the bottom of the pan. When the salt is hot, add the oxtails, and brown them on all sides. (The salt draws out the fat from the oxtails, and they will fry in it.)

2. While the oxtails are browning, assemble the braising liquid ingredients in a 4-quart casserole. Use a slotted spoon to transfer the oxtails to the casserole, draining off extra fat. Stir the oxtails in the liquid until the meat is well coated.

3. Add the onions to the fat in the frying pan or wok, and cook them over medium heat, stirring, until they are translucent. Transfer them to the casserole with a slotted spoon.

4. Bring the liquid in the casserole to a boil over high heat. Reduce heat to medium low, cover the casserole, and simmer the oxtails gently for 4 hours, or until the meat is very tender.

5. Remove the oxtails and onions to a serving dish, again using a slotted spoon, and keep them warm.

6. Skim all fat possible from the liquid in the casserole. Mix the cornstarch and water binder, and stir it into the liquid. Simmer the sauce over medium heat, stirring, for 5 minutes. The sauce will thicken slightly.

7. Stir in the sesame oil. Pour the sauce over the oxtails, or return the oxtails to the casserole if you plan to take it to the table. Serve the stew hot.

Preparation time: 15 minutes
Cooking time: 4 hours
Serves: 4

SWEET-AND-SOUR OXTAILS

Basically, this dish is prepared in the same way as Home-style Sweet-and-Sour Spareribs (see page 166), although the cooking time is much longer. I have served this dish, which is cooked without vegetables, as a part of a five-course Chinese dinner. If you want a one-pot dinner, add carrots and turnips (see Note) or vegetables of your choice during the last hour of cooking. The point at which you add vegetables depends upon what kind of vegetables you choose.

Ingredients

Salt for browning oxtails
3½ pounds oxtails, disjointed and trimmed of surplus fat

Braising Liquid

½   cup black soy sauce
½   cup sherry
¼   cup (packed) brown sugar
1   cup water
2   cloves garlic, peeled and mashed
2   whole star anise

Binder and Final Seasoning

1   teaspoon cornstarch
1   teaspoon cold water
¼   cup cider vinegar
½   teaspoon sesame oil

Instructions

1. Heat a large skillet or a wok over high heat. When the pan is hot, sprinkle in about 1 teaspoon salt. When the salt is hot, add the oxtails, and brown them on all sides.

2. Transfer the oxtails to a 3½-quart casserole, using a slotted spoon to drain them of excess fat.

3. Mix the braising liquid, pour it over the meat, and bring the liquid to a boil. Reduce the heat to low, cover the casserole, and simmer the oxtails for 4 hours, turning them from time to time.

4. Lift the oxtails into a serving dish with a slotted spoon, and keep them hot. Skim the sauce of excess fat.

5. Mix the cornstarch and water binder, and stir it into the braising liquid. Add the vinegar and sesame oil, and simmer the sauce for 5 minutes.

6. Pour the sauce over the oxtails, or return them to the sauce in the casserole, and serve them hot.

Preparation time: 15 minutes
Cooking time: 4 hours
Serves: 4

Note: To turn Sweet-and-Sour Oxtails into a one-pot dinner, peel 3 carrots, and cut them into ½-inch chunks; then peel 2 small turnips, and cut them into ⅛-inch pieces. Add the vegetables to the stew during the last hour of cooking.

CHINESE-STYLE CORNED BEEF AND CABBAGE

Corned beef and cabbage is such an easy dish to cook, and when some soy sauce, star anise, and other seasonings are added to the pot, this familiar dish becomes an outstanding one — with a different flavor.

The accompanying sauce is an invention that isn't authentically Oriental — sour cream isn't used in Chinese cooking — but it goes nicely with the corned beef.

Ingredients

4-pound piece of corned beef brisket

Braising Liquid

2 tablespoons black soy sauce
½ cup sherry
1 teaspoon sugar
2 whole star anise
1 dried chili pepper, broken in half (use both seeds and pod)

Cabbage

1 head green cabbage (about 1½ pounds), cored and cut into 6 wedges

Sauce for Finished Dish

4 teaspoons Dijon-style mustard
1 tablespoon thin soy sauce
½ cup dairy sour cream
1 teaspoon bottled horseradish

Instructions

1. Put the corned beef into a large container, and pour cold water over it. Soak the beef for at least 3 hours, changing the water several times. (This will take the excess saltiness out of the beef.)

2. Drain the meat, and put it into a casserole large enough (4 quarts) to hold the meat, the cabbage, and the braising liquid.

3. Mix the braising liquid, and pour it over the corned beef. Add enough water to cover the meat by 1 to 2 inches.

4. Bring the liquid to a boil, reduce the heat to low, cover the casserole, and simmer the corned beef for about 3 hours, turning it over at the halfway mark (1½ hours).

5. Add the cabbage to the pot. (You will probably have to remove some of the liquid to make room.) Cover the pot, and simmer the beef and cabbage until both are done (45 minutes to 1 hour).

6. Combine the sauce ingredients in a small serving dish, stirring until they are well blended. (Do not heat the sauce.)

7. Remove the cabbage to a serving bowl, using a slotted spoon to drain it well. (If you wish, you can ladle some of the braising liquid over the cabbage to make a soupy dish.)

8. Drain the corned beef, and place it on a platter. Carve the meat across the grain into ¼-inch slices, and serve it at once, with the sour cream sauce and the cabbage.

Preparation time: 3 hours to soak corned beef; 10 minutes or less to prepare cabbage
Cooking time: 3½ to 4 hours
Serves: 6

BRAISED TONGUE IN MUSTARD, WINE, AND SOY SAUCE

Although mustard is commonly used as a dip for Chinese hors d'oeuvres, it is seldom used as a component in the multitude of Chinese sauces. In this dish, Dijon-style mustard is combined with black soy sauce and sherry — with delicious results.

Ingredients

3½-pound fresh beef tongue

Braising Liquid

¼ cup black soy sauce
¼ cup sherry
1 teaspoon sugar
⅔ cup chicken broth
1 dried chili pepper, broken in half (use both seeds and pod)

Binder

1 tablespoon cornstarch
1 tablespoon cold water

Final Seasonings

½ teaspoon sesame oil
1 tablespoon Dijon-style mustard

Instructions

1. Rinse the tongue well under cold running water. Place the tongue in a large casserole, add water to cover it by at least 1 inch, and bring the water to a boil. Reduce the heat to medium low, cover the pot, and simmer the tongue for 1 hour. (This parboiling makes it possible to peel the tongue.)

2. While the tongue is parboiling, assemble the braising liquid ingredients in a 3-quart (or larger) casserole.

3. Drain the tongue in a colander, and rinse it under cold running water until it is cool enough to handle. Slice off any gristly parts of the base, and strip off the skin, using a sharp knife if necessary.

4. Put the tongue into the casserole with the braising liquid, and bring the liquid to a boil over high heat. Reduce the heat to medium low, cover the casserole, and simmer the tongue for 3 hours, turning it over occasionally.

5. Remove the tongue to a serving platter, and cut it into slightly diagonal ¼-inch slices. Keep it warm.

6. Simmer the braising liquid until it is reduced to about 1½ cups.

7. Stir together the cornstarch and water binder, mix it into the liquid, and simmer the sauce for 5 minutes.

8. Mix the sesame oil and mustard in a bowl, and add a little of the reduced cooking liquid to it, whisking to blend well. Add this mixture to the braising liquid in the casserole. Pour the sauce over the tongue, and serve it hot.

Preparation time: 1 hour to parboil and peel the tongue
Cooking time: 3 hours
Serves: 4 or 5

STEWED CALVES' HEARTS

Hearts have a somewhat chewy texture and a nice taste. When braised with an assortment of vegetables, they make a delicious stew.

This is essentially a one-dish meal for four, but if you serve it with rice or noodles and a salad, it will feed six.

Ingredients

Vegetable oil for browning meat and onions
2   calves' hearts, trimmed of fat and gristle and cut into 1-by-2-inch strips
1   large onion, cut in half from top to bottom, peeled, and cut into ¼-inch slices along the grain

Braising Liquid

8-ounce can tomato sauce
¼   cup black soy sauce
¼   cup sherry
½   teaspoon sugar

Vegetables

3   carrots, peeled and cut into 1-inch diagonal chunks
2   ribs of celery, cut into 1-inch diagonal slices
4   small potatoes, peeled and cut into 1-inch chunks

Final Seasoning

½   teaspoon sesame oil

Instructions

1. Put a large, heavy frying pan or a wok over high heat, and pour in enough oil to film the bottom (about 1½ tablespoons); tilt the pan to coat the cooking surface thoroughly. When the oil is hot, add the heart strips and onions, and brown them, stirring them frequently.

2. Mix the braising liquid in a 2½- to 3-quart casserole. Add the browned meat and onions and the carrots, celery, and potatoes, and bring the sauce to a boil over high heat. Reduce the heat to medium low, cover the casserole, and simmer the stew for 1½ hours, or until the meat is done. Stir the ingredients occasionally.

3. Stir in the sesame oil, and serve the stew hot.

Preparation time: 10 minutes
Cooking time: 1½ hours
Serves: 4 to 6

CHICKEN

The chicken, like its barnyard companion the pig, is easy to raise, doesn't need much space, and is relatively inexpensive to feed. It seems to be the most common table meat in so many countries because it is the most inexpensive. Chicken is extremely versatile, blending well with almost any kind of sauce or seasoning.

With the exception of Poached Chicken Breasts with Spicy Peanut Sauce, all the recipes in this chapter call for chicken with bones, either cooked whole or hacked into small pieces. The Chinese understand that the bones impart more flavor to long-simmered dishes.

If you are fortunate enough to live near a Chinatown, you may be able to buy live chickens, because the Chinese demand the freshest food available. If live chickens cannot be had, the chickens in the Chinatown markets are usually very fresh.

POT-ROASTED WHOLE CHICKEN

My childhood memory of chicken every Sunday as a special treat is very strong. If we were eating American food, the chicken would be cut into serving pieces, shaken with seasoned flour in a brown paper bag, and fried in oil in a big cast-iron skillet. The oil was drained, and cream was poured over the chicken and reduced. If we were eating Chinese food, a pot-roasted whole chicken was served. In Cantonese, it is called whut gai.

Ingredients

4 dried black Oriental mushrooms
6 golden needles (dried lily buds)
6 dried black wood ears
 Vegetable oil for browning chicken
 3½-to 4-pound frying chicken, whole
1 medium-sized onion, cut in half from top to bottom, peeled, and cut into ¼-inch slices along the grain
 Dried tangerine peel, a piece the size of a fifty-cent piece

Braising Liquid

¼ cup thin soy sauce
¼ cup sherry
½ teaspoon sugar
2 cloves garlic, peeled and flattened
1 slice fresh ginger root, ⅛-inch thick, flattened
½ cup water (or chicken broth)

Binder and Final Seasoning

1½ teaspoons cornstarch
1½ teaspoons cold water
½ teaspoon sesame oil

Garnish

 Sprigs of fresh coriander (or parsley)

Instructions

1. In separate bowls, soak the black mushrooms, golden needles, and wood ears in warm water for 1 hour. Then drain, stem, and quarter the mushrooms. Drain the golden needles, squeeze them dry, and tie a knot in each one. Rinse all grit from the wood ears, and drain them.

2. Put a large frying pan or a wok over high heat, and pour in about 1½ tablespoons of oil, tilting the pan to cover the cooking surface. When the oil is hot, put the chicken in the pan, and brown it on all sides, turning it often. Lower the heat if the skin starts to burn.

3. Transfer the chicken, breast side down, to a casserole large enough (4 quarts) to hold it. Add the mushrooms, golden needles, wood ears, onion, and tangerine peel to the pan, and sauté everything until the onion slices are translucent.

4. Drain any excess oil from the frying pan, and add the braising liquid ingredients. Mix well, and bring to a boil.

5. Pour the liquid over the chicken. Cover the casserole, and simmer the chicken over low heat for 1 hour, or until done, turning it several times so that all sides are cooked. If the braising liquid seems to be cooking away too fast, add more thin soy sauce, sherry, and water in equal parts.

6. When chicken is done, transfer it to a platter. (Test for doneness by piercing the thigh; the juices should run clear.) Discard the slice of ginger.

7. Mix the cornstarch and water binder, and stir it into the liquid. Cook the sauce for a few minutes to thicken it.

8. Stir in the sesame oil, and pour the sauce over the chicken or serve it separately. Garnish the chicken with the sprigs of fresh coriander or parsley, and serve it hot.

Preparation time: 1 hour
Cooking time: 1 to 1¼ hours
Serves: 4 as a main course, 6 to 8 as part of a Chinese meal

SZECHUAN CHICKEN AND PEANUTS IN BROWN SAUCE

The quantity of dried chili peppers used will determine how fiery this dish will be. The recipe is middle-of-the-road spicy; add more peppers if you like your food hot. You can substitute pine nuts, walnuts, or cashews for the peanuts.

Ingredients

6   dried black Oriental mushrooms

Braising Liquid

2   tablespoons thin soy sauce
2   tablespoons sherry
¼   teaspoon sugar
3   tablespoons hoisin sauce
1   tablespoon ground brown bean sauce
1   tablespoon vinegar (rice, cider, or white)
2   cloves garlic, peeled and flattened
1   slice fresh ginger root, ⅛ inch thick, flattened
2   dried chili peppers, broken in half (use both seeds and pods)
¼   cup mushroom-soaking liquid (see step 1)

Chicken and Vegetables

Vegetable oil for browning chicken and onions
3- to 3½-pound frying chicken, cut into small pieces
(see page 36)
1   large onion, cut in half from top to bottom, peeled, and cut into ¼-inch slices along the grain
¼   cup bamboo shoots, sliced about ⅛ inch thick and cut into ½-by-2 inch pieces.
⅓   cup roasted salted peanuts, strained to remove excess salt

Binder and Final Seasoning

2   teaspoons cornstarch

2 teaspoons cold water
½ teaspoon sesame oil

Garnish

1 scallion, cut into ¼-inch rounds (use both white and green parts) (or fresh coriander leaves)

Instructions

1. Cover the mushrooms with warm water, and soak them for 1 hour. Drain the mushrooms, reserving the soaking liquid. Cut off and discard stems, and cut the caps into quarters.

2. Mix the braising liquid in a casserole large enough (3½ to 4 quarts) to hold all the chicken and vegetables.

3. Heat a heavy cast-iron skillet or a wok over high heat until the pan is hot. Pour enough oil (about 1½ tablespoons) into the pan, tilting the pan to coat thoroughly. When the oil is hot, add half the chicken pieces and brown them, turning them as necessary (8 to 10 minutes). Transfer the browned pieces with a slotted spoon to the casserole, leaving behind any excess oil. Throw in the onions and mushrooms with the last batch of chicken as it browns. When the chicken is browned, transfer it, with the vegetables, to the casserole. Again, use a slotted spoon. Mix all the ingredients well.

4. Bring the braising liquid to a boil; then reduce the heat to medium low, cover the casserole, and simmer the chicken for 15 minutes. Add the bamboo shoots and peanuts, mix well. Simmer for another 20 minutes. Then discard the ginger slice.

5. Mix the cornstarch and water binder, and stir it into the liquid. Cook the sauce for a few minutes to thicken.

6. Add the sesame oil, and give everything a final stir. Sprinkle the scallions or coriander over the chicken, and serve hot.

Preparation time: 1 hour to soak mushrooms; 20 minutes to brown chicken
Cooking time: 40 minutes
Serves: 4

POACHED CHICKEN BREASTS WITH SPICY PEANUT SAUCE

There is a cold noodle dish served in Peking that is very popular in the summer. It is sauced with a mixture of Chinese sesame paste, vinegar, wine, and other seasonings. I find the sesame paste quite strong and use peanut butter instead. The result is pleasant indeed. You can make the dish spicier by using more chili oil (or Tabasco) to taste. Why am I talking about a noodle dish when this is a recipe for chicken breasts? Because I use the noodle sauce (minus the noodles) on the chicken!

Ingredients

2   whole chicken breasts (4 sections altogether), boned and skinned

Poaching Liquid

2   tablespoons black soy sauce
¼   cup sherry
½   teaspoon sugar
2   cloves garlic, peeled and flattened
1   slice fresh ginger root, ⅛-inch thick, flattened
½   teaspoon sesame oil
2   whole star anise

Peanut Sauce

4   tablespoons peanut butter
1   teaspoon thin soy sauce
1   tablespoon sherry
½   teaspoon sugar
2   tablespoons rice vinegar
¼   teaspoon chili oil (or to taste) (or Tabasco)
¼   cup chicken broth

Instructions

1. Split the chicken breasts in half lengthwise so that you have four pieces. Place them in a shallow casserole large enough (10 inches in diameter) to hold them in a single layer.

2. Mix all the ingredients for the poaching liquid, and pour it over the chicken breasts. Now add enough water to cover the chicken. Swirl the casserole around to mix the liquid thoroughly.

3. Remove the chicken breasts to a plate. Bring the poaching liquid to a boil, then return the chicken breasts to the casserole. Reduce the heat to medium low, cover the casserole, and simmer the chicken for about 8 minutes. Turn the chicken pieces over, and simmer them for another 8 minutes. Do not overcook the chicken breasts. (To test for doneness, pierce the thickest part of the chicken breast with the point of a knife. If the inside is still pink, cook the chicken a little longer.) The exact cooking time depends upon the size of the breasts.

4. Meanwhile, make the peanut sauce by combining all the ingredients with a wire whisk. (The mixture will be somewhat stiff.)

5. Remove the chicken breasts from the poaching liquid with a slotted spoon, and place them on a serving platter. (You can cut the chicken breasts into thin slices across the grain, if you wish, or leave them whole.) To serve cold, let the chicken cool; then pour the peanut sauce over it. To serve hot, heat the peanut sauce before pouring it over the hot chicken.

Preparation time: 15 to 20 minutes
Cooking time: 20 to 25 minutes
Serves: 4

PLUM SAUCE CHICKEN WITH BLACK MUSHROOMS AND PINE NUTS

There is a Chinese product called plum sauce that is similar to the bottled chutney one finds in supermarkets. This recipe uses either plum sauce or chutney in the cooking liquid for the chicken instead of calling for it on the side as a relish. The chicken is even better reheated the next day.

Ingredients

6   dried black Oriental mushrooms
    Vegetable oil for browning chicken and onions
    3-to-4-pound frying chicken, cut into small pieces
    (see page 36)
1   medium-sized onion, cut in half from top to bottom, peeled, and cut into ¼-inch slices along the grain

Braising Liquid

2   tablespoons thin soy sauce
2   tablespoons sherry
½   teaspoon sugar
2   cloves garlic, peeled and flattened
1   slice fresh ginger root, ⅛-inch thick, flattened
½   cup mushroom-soaking liquid (see step 1)
½   cup plum sauce, fruits chopped coarsely (or chutney)
2   tablespoons tomato catsup
3   dried chili peppers, broken in half (use both seeds and pods)
2   whole star anise

Binder and Final Seasonings

1   teaspoon cornstarch
1   teaspoon water

¼ cup pine nuts
½ teaspoon sesame oil

Instructions

1. Soak the mushrooms for 1 hour in warm water to cover them. Drain the mushrooms, and reserve the soaking liquid. Remove and discard the stems. Cut the caps into sixths.

2. Put a large frying pan or a wok over high heat, and pour in enough oil to coat the cooking surface (about 1½ tablespoons), tilting the pan to distribute the oil. When the oil is hot, add half the chicken pieces to the pan, and brown them on all sides (about 8 minutes).

3. While the first batch of chicken is browning, mix the braising liquid in a 3½- or 4-quart casserole. Transfer the browned chicken to the casserole, using a slotted spoon to drain the pieces of any excess oil. Brown the second batch of chicken, and add the onions and mushrooms to the pan. Drain the chicken and vegetables, and mix them into the casserole.

4. Bring the braising liquid to a boil over high heat, reduce the heat to medium low, cover the casserole, and simmer the chicken for 45 minutes to 1 hour, turning the chicken pieces once or twice. Then discard the slice of ginger.

5. Mix the cornstarch and water binder, and stir it into the liquid. Cook the sauce for a few minutes until it is very lightly thickened.

6. Stir in pine nuts; then add the sesame oil, and give everything a final stir. Serve the chicken hot.

Preparation time: 1 hour to soak mushrooms; 15 to 20 minutes to brown the chicken
Cooking time: 1¼ hours
Serves: 4

WHITE-HACKED CHICKEN

The chicken you use for this recipe must be <u>very</u> fresh because the success of the dish depends upon the real chicken flavor coming out. It would be ideal to get a freshly killed chicken, but that is becoming almost impossible. However, if you live near a Chinatown or a kosher butcher, you should be able to get truly fresh chickens. You can make this dish ahead of time, refrigerate it until serving time, and serve it either cold or at room temperature. This poached chicken is elegant in its simplicity.

Ingredients

3½- to 4-pound frying chicken, very fresh, cleaned and left whole

Poaching Liquid

2 cloves garlic, peeled and flattened
1 slice fresh ginger root, ⅛-inch thick, flattened

Final Seasoning

Sesame oil to rub on cooked chicken

Dips

Dip 1: Oyster sauce
Dip 2: Sesame oil mixed with thin soy sauce and grated fresh
       ginger root to taste
Dip 3: Chili oil (or Tabasco) mixed with thin soy sauce and rice
       vinegar to taste

Garnishes

Fresh coriander leaves (optional)
Scallion rounds, thinly cut

Instructions

1. Put the chicken into a casserole large enough (5 to 6 quarts) to accommodate it, and add ample cold water to cover it. Remove the chicken, and set it aside. Add the garlic and ginger to the water.

2. Cover the casserole, and bring the poaching liquid to a boil over high heat. Gently ease the chicken into the boiling liquid. Bring the liquid back to a boil, and cover the casserole. Turn the heat to lowest setting, and simmer the chicken for about 1 hour. To check to see if the chicken is done, cut into the thigh at the thickest part to see if the juices run clear. If they are still pink, cook the chicken a little longer. Do not overcook. (Cantonese like White-hacked Chicken just this side of undercooked.) Another way of cooking this chicken is to bring the liquid to a boil, put the chicken into it, bring the liquid back to a boil, cover the casserole, turn off the heat, and let the chicken sit for 3 or 4 hours, until cold. This second method conserves fuel.

3. When chicken is done (by the first cooking method), put it into a colander, and set it under cold running water until it is cool. (This stops further cooking.) If you have let the chicken cook in the broth (the second method), omit this step.

4. Pat the chicken dry with paper towels. Rub its entire surface with sesame oil. Cut the wings and legs off. Then proceed to hack the chicken into pieces measuring about 1½ by 2½ inches, using a sharp cleaver (see page 36) Place the pieces neatly on a platter. Garnish the chicken with coriander leaves and scallion rounds and serve.

Preparation time: 10 minutes
Cooking time: About 1 hour
Serves: 4 as a main course, 8 or more as part of a Chinese meal, 10 as an hors d'oeuvre

CURRIED CHICKEN WITH VEGETABLES

Curried chicken is a very popular family-style dish among the Cantonese. This version, with its assortment of vegetables, makes a complete dinner.

Braising Liquid

2 tablespoons thin soy sauce
2 tablespoons sherry
¼ teaspoon sugar
2 cloves garlic, peeled and mashed
1 slice fresh ginger root, ⅛-inch thick, flattened
2 tablespoons curry powder (or to taste)
¼ teaspoon chili powder (or to taste)
2 tablespoons tomato catsup
½ cup chicken broth

Chicken and Vegetables

Vegetable oil for browning chicken and onions
3- to 3½-pound frying chicken, cut into small pieces (see page 36)
large onion, cut in half from top to bottom, peeled, and cut into ¼-inch slices along the grain
2 carrots, peeled and sliced diagonally into ¼-inch pieces
2 ribs celery, sliced diagonally into ½-inch cubes
2 medium-sized potatoes, peeled and cut into ½-inch cubes

Binder and Final Seasoning

2 teaspoons cornstarch
2 teaspoons cold water
½ teaspoon sesame oil

Garnish

Fresh coriander leaves (or fresh parsley)

Instructions

1. Mix the braising liquid ingredients in a casserole large enough (3½ or 4 quarts) to hold the chicken and all the vegetables.

2. Heat a heavy cast-iron skillet or a wok. When the pan is hot, pour about 1½ tablespoons of oil into it, swirling the oil to coat the cooking surface. When the oil is hot, add half the chicken pieces and all the onion slices, and brown them, stirring (about 5 minutes). Transfer the chicken and onion to the casserole with a slotted spoon, leaving any excess oil in the frying pan.

3. Brown the remaining chicken, and while doing so, add the carrots, celery, and potatoes to the pan. When chicken has browned, transfer everything to the casserole, and stir to make sure that all the ingredients are well coated with the braising liquid.

4. Bring the liquid to a boil; then reduce the heat to medium low, cover the casserole, and simmer the chicken for 25 to 30 minutes. At the halfway point, shift the chicken and vegetables on the bottom of the casserole to the top and vice versa. Discard the slice of ginger. Cook for another 10 to 15 minutes.

5. Mix the cornstarch and water binder, and stir it into the braising liquid. Cook the sauce for a few minutes to allow it to thicken slightly.

6. Add the sesame oil, and sprinkle the coriander leaves on top. Serve the curried chicken hot.

Preparation time: 15 minutes
Cooking time: 40 to 45 minutes
Serves: 4

DEVILED CHICKEN WINGS

Chicken wings have always been a great favorite with the Chinese, who think this part of the bird is particularly tasty. Chicken wings used to be very inexpensive, but now they are sometimes as expensive per pound as a whole chicken. I would recommend serving Deviled Chicken Wings as an hors d'oeuvre or as part of a multiple-course Chinese dinner. They are also good cold for picnics.

Ingredients

1½ pounds chicken wings (8 to 10, depending upon size)

Braising Liquid

3   tablespoons black soy sauce
¼   cup sherry
½   teaspoon sugar.
1   clove garlic, peeled and flattened
1   slice fresh ginger root, ⅛-inch thick, flattened
1½ dried chili peppers, broken in half (use both seed and pods)
¼   cup water

Binder and Final Seasonings

1½ teaspoons cornstarch
1½ teaspoons water
½   teaspoon sesame oil
1   tablespoon Dijon-style mustard

Instructions

1. Disjoint the chicken wings. Freeze the tips if you wish to use them for stock, otherwise discard.

2. Mix the braising liquid ingredients in a 2-quart casserole, and bring the liquid to a boil over high heat.

3. Add the wings to the pot, and mix them with the liquid. Reduce the heat to medium low, cover the casserole, and simmer the chicken wings for 10 to 15 minutes. Turn the wings over, and simmer them 10 to 15 minutes longer. Then discard the ginger slice.

4. Stir the cornstarch and water binder, and mix it into the liquid. Cook the sauce for a few minutes until it has thickened slightly.

5. Pour about ¼ cup of the sauce into a small bowl, and stir in the sesame oil and mustard with a whisk. Pour this mixture back into the casserole, and stir everything together until the sauce is thoroughly blended. Serve the chicken wings hot.

Preparation time: 15 minutes
Cooking time: 30 to 40 minutes
Serves: 4 to 8 as a first course or as part of a Chinese meal

TANGY CHICKEN WINGS

There is a pecking order in Chinese families at mealtime. The oldest male gets the choicest piece of meat; the others are served in descending order, according to age and gender (males first, females last). Whenever we had chicken, I, being the youngest girl in the family, got the neck and the gizzard. Once in a while, as a treat, I would get a chicken wing. Now when I buy chicken from the butcher, I automatically throw away the neck. However, I do still eat the gizzard, and I really like the wings better than any part of the chicken. I serve this dish as an hors d'oeuvre; it's not substantial enough to be a main course.

Ingredients

Vegetable oil for browning chicken
1 pound chicken wings (6 to 8, depending upon size)

Braising Liquid

2 tablespoons thin soy sauce
2 tablespoons sherry
½ teaspoon sugar
1 clove garlic, peeled and flattened
1 slice fresh ginger root, ⅛-inch thick, flattened
2 dried chili peppers, broken in half (use both seeds and pods)
1 tablespoon rice vinegar (or white vinegar)
1 tablespoon tomato catsup
¼ cup chicken broth (or water)

Binder and Final Seasoning

1 teaspoon cornstarch
1 teaspoon water
¼ teaspoon sesame oil

Garnish

2 scallions, trimmed and cut into ¼-inch rounds

Instructions

1. Disjoint the chicken wings. Freeze the tips if you wish to use them for stock; otherwise discard.

2. Put a large, heavy frying pan or a wok over high heat. Pour about 1½ tablespoons of oil into the hot pan, and tilt the pan so that the cooking surface is coated. When the oil is hot, add the chicken wings to the pan, and brown them on all sides (about 7 to 10 minutes).

3. While the wings are browning, mix the braising liquid ingredients in a 2-quart casserole. Transfer the browned wings to the casserole; use a slotted spoon for this to drain them of excess oil.

4. Bring the braising liquid to a boil over high heat. Reduce the heat to medium low, cover the casserole, and simmer the chicken wings about 40 minutes, turning them once or twice. Then discard the ginger slice.

5. Stir the cornstarch and water binder together, and mix it into the liquid. Cook the sauce for a few minutes to thicken it slightly.

6. Stir in the sesame oil. Sprinkle the scallion rounds over the chicken wings, and serve them hot.

Preparation time: 10 to 15 minutes
Cooking time: About 40 minutes
Serves: 3 or 4 as an appetizer

PINEAPPLE CHICKEN WINGS

There is a saying, "The closer to the bone, the sweeter the meat." I suppose that's why chicken wings are so tasty: They're mostly bone.

Ingredients

Vegetable oil for browning chicken
1   pound (6 to 8) chicken wings

Braising Liquid

1   tablespoon black soy sauce
3   tablespoons sherry
2   tablespoons dark brown sugar
¼   cup reserved pineapple syrup
2   dried chili peppers, broken in half (use both seeds and pods)
3   tablespoons cider vinegar

Pineapple

1   cup canned pineapple chunks, drained (reserve syrup)

Binder and Final Seasoning

2   teaspoons cornstarch
2   teaspoons water
¼   teaspoon sesame oil

Garnish

Fresh coriander leaves (or scallion rounds)

Instructions

1. Disjoint the chicken wings. Freeze the tips if you wish to use them for stock; otherwise discard.

2. Set a skillet or a wok over high heat. When it is hot, add enough oil (about 1½ tablespoons) to film the pan, tilting it to coat the cooking surface thoroughly. When the oil is hot, add the chicken wings, and brown them on all sides (7 to 10 minutes). Using a slotted spoon, transfer them to a 2-quart casserole; drain the wings of excess oil.

3. Add all the braising liquid ingredients to the casserole. Bring the liquid to a boil, reduce the heat to medium low, cover the casserole, and simmer the wings for 10 to 15 minutes. Add the pineapple chunks, and simmer the ingredients 10 to 15 minutes longer, or until the wings are done. (To test for doneness, cut into the thickest part of the wing; the juices should run clear.)

4. Stir together the cornstarch and water binder, and add it to the braising liquid. Cook the sauce for a few minutes to thicken it.

5. Add the sesame oil, and give all the ingredients a final stir. Sprinkle the coriander leaves over the chicken wings, and serve them hot.

Preparation time: 10 minutes
Cooking time: 30 to 40 minutes
Serves: 3 or 4 as an appetizer, 6 or more as part of a Chinese meal

STEWED CHICKEN WITH DRIED CHESTNUTS

Although the water chestnut is always associated with Chinese cooking, the regular chestnut almost never is. Yet, archaeological excavations of tombs dating from the early Han dynasty have turned up food remains that include chestnuts. It is thought that the Liang-hsing District in Hopei Province has the best-quality chestnuts. Vendors in northern China roast chestnuts by burying them in very hot sand.

This recipe calls for dried chestnuts, which have a delicately smoky taste.

Ingredients

1   cup dried chestnuts

Braising Liquid

2   tablespoons thin soy sauce
2   tablespoons sherry
1   teaspoon sugar
2   cloves garlic, peeled and flattened
1   slice fresh ginger root, ⅛-inch thick, flattened
2   tablespoons oyster sauce
¼   teaspoon white pepper
½   cup chicken broth

Chicken

Vegetable oil for browning chicken
3- to 3½-pound frying chicken, cut into pieces (see page 36)

Binder and Final Seasoning

2   teaspoons cornstarch
2   teaspoons cold water
½   teaspoon sesame oil

Garnish

Sprigs of fresh coriander (or fresh parsley)

Instructions

1. Cover the dried chestnuts with water, refrigerate, and soak them for 24 hours. Drain the chestnuts, removing any bits of skin, and simmer them in fresh water for 45 to 60 minutes, until not quite done.

2. Mix the braising liquid ingredients in a 3½- to 4-quart casserole.

3. Heat a large skillet or a wok over high heat, and add about 1½ tablespoons of oil, tilting the pan to film the cooking surface evenly. When the oil is hot, add half the chicken pieces, and brown them on all sides (about 8 minutes). Add the browned chicken pieces to the braising liquid, transferring them to the casserole with a slotted spoon to drain them of excess oil. Brown the rest of the chicken, adding a little more oil if needed, and transfer the browned pieces to the casserole, again using a slotted spoon.

4. Drain the simmered chestnuts, add them to the casserole, and mix everything well. Bring the braising liquid to a boil over high heat. Reduce the heat to medium low, cover the casserole, and simmer the chicken and chestnuts for about 1 hour, or until both are done, turning the chicken pieces once. Then discard the slice of ginger.

5. Mix the cornstarch and water binder, and stir it into the braising liquid. Cook the sauce for a few minutes to allow it to thicken slightly.

6. Add the sesame oil, and give everything a final stir. Garnish the chicken with the fresh coriander or parsley, and serve it hot.

Preparation time: 24 hours to soak chestnuts; 1 hour to simmer the chestnuts
Cooking time: 1 hour
Serves: 4 as a main course, 6 to 8 as part of a Chinese meal

SALT-COOKED CHICKEN

The Chinese way of cooking a chicken in hot salt gives you a tender, unusually moist bird that has a delicious, vaguely smoky taste. The only time I recall my mother using a wok was when she cooked chicken this way; a wok was the only utensil large enough to hold the several pounds of salt needed to surround and cover the chicken. A four-quart French oval cocotte is a good casserole to use, as is a large Dutch oven — or even a wok.

Kosher salt is better than ordinary table salt for preparing the chicken because it is coarser and because you don't need as much of it as you would if you were using the finer salt.

Marinade

2   tablespoons thin soy sauce
2   tablespoons sherry
¼   teaspoon sugar
2   cloves garlic, peeled and flattened
1   slice fresh ginger root, ⅛-inch thick, flattened
½   teaspoon sesame oil

Ingredients

4-to-6 pounds coarse (kosher) salt
3½-to 4-pound frying chicken, cleaned and left whole
Brown paper bag to encase chicken

Instructions

1. Mix the marinade, and marinate the chicken in it at room temperature for a least 1 hour, turning it from time to time.

2. Put half the salt in the pot you will be using. (The amount will depend upon the size and shape of the utensil.) Heat the salt over the medium high heat until it is red-hot (20 to 30 minutes). At the same time, heat the remaining salt in a frying pan until it, too, is red-hot.

3. Drain the chicken, and pat it dry with paper towels. Put the chicken in the brown paper bag, which should fit rather snugly, and twist the open end of the bag closed.

4. Put the chicken in the pot of hot salt, breast side down, and wiggle it around in the salt, leaving at least 1½ inches of salt between it and the bottom of the pot. Pour the second batch of hot salt over the chicken so that it is completely buried. Cover the casserole, and cook the chicken over moderate heat for about 1 hour, or until it is done. (Checking to see whether the chicken is done can be a pain in the neck because, in opening the bag and taking the chicken out to see if the juices run clear when the thigh is pricked, you will probably spill salt all over the stove and floor.) If the chicken needs further cooking, fasten the bag again and rebury the bird in the salt.

5. When chicken is done, take it out of the paper bag, and put it on a platter. (It is very possible that parts of the chicken will stick to the bag. It is also possible that the chicken will be so tender that it will fall apart. In any case, it will be succulent.) Serve it hot.

Preparation time: 1 hour
Cooking time: About 2 hours
Serves: 2 as a main course, 4 to 6 as part of a Chinese meal

Note: Juices from the chicken will probably seep through the paper bag and discolor the salt. The salt at the bottom of the pot will also turn gray or brown. Save any salt that is reasonably clear, and reuse it when you make this dish again or for preparing Piquant Salt-baked Cornish Hens (see page 224).

SIZZLING CHICKEN IN GRAVY

There is a little restaurant on Grant Avenue in San Francisco called Bow Hon that features clay pot cooking. This is my version of one of their specialties.

Ingredients

Vegetable oil to cook onions and brown chicken
1   large onion, peeled, halved from top to bottom, and cut into ¼-inch slices along the grain
3- to 3½-pound frying chicken, cut into small pieces (see page 36)

Braising Liquid

2   tablespoons thin soy sauce
2   tablespoons sherry
2   tablespoons oyster sauce
¼   teaspoon sugar
2   cloves garlic, peeled and flattened
1   slice of fresh ginger root, ⅛-inch thick, flattened
½   cup chicken broth

Binder and Final Seasoning

2   teaspoons cornstarch
2   teaspoons cold water
¼   teaspoon sesame oil
Fresh coriander leaves (or 1 scallion, both green and white parts, cut into ¼-inch rounds) (optional)

Instructions

1. Set a heavy cast-iron skillet or a wok over high heat. When the pan is hot, add about 1½ tablespoons of oil, and swirl the pan around to make sure that the cooking surface is coated. When the oil is hot, add the onions, and cook them quickly, stirring, until they become translucent. Do not brown them.

2. Transfer the onions to a casserole large enough (3½ to 4 quarts) to hold the chicken; use a slotted spoon for this to drain any excess oil back into the frying pan. Line the bottom of the casserole with the onions.

3. If needed, add 1 tablespoon of oil to the frying pan. When the oil is hot, add half the chicken pieces, and brown them on all sides over high heat (7 to 10 minutes). Transfer the chicken to the casserole with the slotted spoon, draining excess oil. Brown the remaining chicken pieces, and transfer them to the casserole, again draining any excess oil.

4. Mix the braising liquid ingredients well, and pour the liquid over the chicken. Bring the braising liquid to a boil, reduce the heat to medium low, cover the casserole, and simmer the chicken for 45 minutes, turning the pieces at the halfway mark so that the pieces on the bottom are switched to the top and vice versa. Then discard the slice of ginger.

5. Stir together the cornstarch and water binder, and mix it into the casserole. Cook the chicken for a few minutes until the sauce thickens slightly.

6. Drizzle the sesame oil over the chicken, and give everything a final stir. Sprinkle the coriander leaves or scallions over the chicken, and serve it hot.

Preparation time: 15 minutes
Cooking time: About 1 hour
Serves: 3 or 4

OYSTER SAUCE CHICKEN LEGS

Chicken legs are always a nice item for a picnic or a hot or cold buffet. If you are tired of the same old fried chicken, this recipe will give you an interesting variation.

Ingredients

Vegetable oil for browning chicken
8   chicken legs (drumsticks and thighs), disjointed

Braising Liquid

3   tablespoons thin soy sauce
6   tablespoons sherry
½   teaspoon sugar
2   cloves garlic, peeled and flattened
1   slice fresh ginger root, ⅛-inch thick, flattened
¼   teaspoon white pepper
3   tablespoons oyster sauce
¼   cup chicken broth

Binder and Final Seasoning

1   teaspoon cornstarch
1   teaspoon cold water
½   teaspoon sesame oil
2   scallions, cut into ¼-inch rounds (use both green and white parts) (or 1½ teaspoons snipped fresh or freeze-dried chives)

Instructions

1. Heat a large, heavy skillet or a wok over high heat; then add about 1½ tablespoons of oil, and swirl the pan to coat the cooking surface thoroughly.

2. When the oil is hot, place the drumsticks and thighs in the pan, and brown them, turning them on all sides (about 10 minutes). (This may have to be done in two batches, depending upon the size of your pan and the size of the chicken legs.)

3. While the legs are being browned, mix the braising liquid ingredients in a 3½- or 4-quart casserole. Bring the liquid to a boil over high heat. Transfer the chicken legs to the casserole with a slotted spoon, making sure to drain them of excess oil. Turn the pieces until they are well coated with the liquid. Reduce the heat to low, cover the casserole, and simmer the chicken legs for 45 to 50 minutes, or until they are done. Then discard the ginger slice.

4. Stir the cornstarch and water binder together, and mix it into the braising liquid. Cook the sauce for a few minutes to thicken it slightly.

5. Add the sesame oil and scallions, and give all the ingredients a final stir. Serve the chicken legs hot.

Preparation time: 10 minutes
Cooking time: 1 hour
Serves: 4 as a main course, 8 as part of a Chinese meal

CHICKEN AND PEPPERS WITH BLACK BEAN, GARLIC, AND EGG SAUCE

The pungency of a black bean and garlic sauce can change a mundane dish to a dazzling one. The sauce for Lobster Cantonese is made with black beans and garlic plus egg and bits of minced pork, and Shrimp with Lobster Sauce (which has no lobster in it) has the same sauce as Lobster Cantonese. This dish of chicken and peppers might therefore be called Chicken with Lobster Sauce without Pork.

Ingredients

Vegetable oil for browning chicken
3- to 3½-pound frying chicken, cut into small pieces (see page 36)
1 large onion, cut in half from top to bottom, peeled, and cut into ¼-inch slices along the grain
3 cloves garlic, peeled and finely minced
2 tablespoons salted black beans, rinsed in water, drained, and mashed

Braising Liquid

2 tablespoons thin soy sauce
4 tablespoons sherry
¼ teaspoon sugar
⅛ teaspoon grated fresh ginger root
½ cup chicken broth

Peppers

2 green peppers, seeded and cut from top to bottom into slices ¼ to ½ inch thick

Binder and Final Seasoning

2	teaspoons cornstarch
2	teaspoons cold water
2	eggs, lightly beaten
½	teaspoon sesame oil

Instructions

1. Heat a large cast-iron frying pan or a wok over high heat, and pour in about 1½ tablespoons of oil. Swirl the oil around so that the cooking surface is coated.

2. Add half the chicken pieces, half the onion slices, half the garlic, and half the black beans. Stir the food to keep it from scorching, and brown the chicken (about 8 minutes).

3. Meanwhile, mix the braising liquid ingredients in a casserole large enough (about 4 quarts) to hold all the ingredients. Bring the sauce to a boil; then turn off the heat.

4. Transfer the sautéed ingredients to the casserole, using a slotted spoon to drain all excess oil. Brown the remaining chicken, onions, black beans and garlic and transfer them to the casserole. Bring the liquid to a boil over high heat. Immediately reduce the heat to low, cover the casserole, and simmer the stew for 40 minutes.

5. Add the green peppers and stir the chicken so that the top pieces go to the bottom and vice versa. Cover the casserole, and simmer for another 10 to 15 minutes.

6. Prepare the cornstarch and water binder, and add it to the liquid. Cook the sauce to thicken slightly. Then stir in the lightly beaten eggs. Let eggs coagulate.

7. Drizzle the sesame oil over the dish, give everything a final stir, and serve the chicken hot.

Preparation time: 15 to 20 minutes
Cooking time: 1 hour
Serves: 4

CHICKEN WITH ORANGE FLAVOR

Once when I was having lunch at a Szechuan restaurant in New York's Chinatown, the waiters distributed tangerines to the customers at the end of the meal. I was charmed by this pleasant surprise. As soon as I had finished peeling the tangerine, the waiter swooped by and gathered the tangerine peel. I then realized this was a way of getting the clientele to help them with their work; they needed the peels for their version of Chicken with Orange Flavor.

Ingredients

Peel of 1 tangerine (or 1 small orange)
Vegetable oil for browning chicken and onions
3- to 3½-pound frying chicken, cut into small pieces (see page 36)
1   large onion, cut in half from top to bottom, peeled, and cut into ¼-inch slices along the grain

Vegetables

¼   cup sliced bamboo shoots (slices should be 2 inches by ½ inch and ⅛ inch thick)
¼   pound snow peas, stemmed and cut in half diagonally

Braising Liquid

4   teaspoons thin soy sauce
4   teaspoons sherry
¼   teaspoon sugar
2   cloves garlic, peeled and flattened
1   slice fresh ginger root, ¼-inch thick, flattened
3   tablespoons hoisin suace
3   dried chili peppers, broken in half (use both seeds and pods)
2   tablespoons vinegar
¼   cup chicken broth

Binder and Final Seasoning

2   teaspoons cornstarch
2   teaspoons cold water
½   teaspoon sesame oil

Instructions

1. If you do not have dried tangerine peel on hand, start 24 hours ahead of time, and set out the stripped-off tangerine peel to dry. Choose a warm spot, such as a turned-off oven heated by a pilot light or the top of a not-too-hot radiator.

2. Put a large frying pan or a wok over high heat. Pour about 1½ tablespoons of oil into the pan, swirling it to coat the cooking surface. When the oil is hot, add half the chicken pieces. Brown the chicken (about 7 to 8 minutes); then transfer the pieces to a 3½- or 4-quart casserole, using a slotted spoon to drain them of any excess oil. Brown the remaining chicken with the onions. Add more oil if necessary. Transfer the chicken and the onions to the casserole, again draining off excess oil.

3. Combine the braising liquid ingredients, including the tangerine peel, and pour the mixture over the chicken and onions. Bring the liquid to a boil, reduce the heat to medium low, cover the casserole, and simmer the chicken for 20 minutes. Add the bamboo shoots, and turn the chicken pieces over. Simmer the ingredients for another 20 minutes. Discard the ginger.

4. Add the snow peas. Immediately prepare the cornstarch and water binder, and mix this into the liquid.

5. Add the sesame oil, and stir all the ingredients. Simmer the chicken for a few minutes so that the sauce has a chance to thicken slightly. Serve the chicken hot.

Preparation time: 24 hours to dry the tangerine peel; 15 minutes to assemble the ingredients
Cooking time: 45 minutes
Serves: 4

CASHEW NUT CHICKEN

Chicken with walnuts or cashew nuts has always been regarded as a very special dish — almost banquet fare — that can be cooked at home instead of being ordered specially from a restaurant. In this it's unlike Peking Duck, which many Chinese feel belongs completely in the realm of restaurant cooking. When served at a banquet, the chicken is boned; in this version, it is not.

Ingredients

5   dried black Oriental mushrooms
     Vegetable oil for browning onions and chicken
1   large onion, cut in half from top to bottom, peeled, and cut into ¼-inch slices along the grain
     3- to 3½-pound frying chicken, cut into small pieces (see page 36)

Braising Liquid

1   tablespoon thin soy sauce
3   tablespoons sherry
3   tablespoons oyster sauce
¼   teaspoon sugar
¼   teaspoon white pepper
2   cloves garlic, peeled and flattened
1   slice fresh ginger root, ⅛-inch thick, flattened
½   cup mushroom-soaking liquid (see step 1)

Vegetables

5   water chestnuts, sliced into ⅛-inch rounds
½   cup cashew nuts (if salted, strained to get rid of excess salt)
¼   pound fresh snow peas, stemmed

Binder and Final Seasoning

2	teaspoons cornstarch
2	teaspoons cold water
½	teaspoon sesame oil

Instructions

1. Cover mushrooms with tepid water, and soak them for 1 hour. Drain the mushrooms, reserving the soaking liquid, squeeze out the surplus water, cut off and discard the stems, and cut the caps into quarters.

2. Heat a large frying pan or a wok, and pour in about 1½ tablespoons of oil, swirling it to cover the cooking surface. When the oil is hot, add the onions, and fry them over medium heat, stirring, until they are translucent. Transfer the onions to line the bottom of a 3- or 4-quart casserole, using a slotted spoon to drain any excess oil.

3. Put 1 tablespoon of oil into the pan, and brown half the chicken pieces (5 to 6 minutes on each side). Drain chicken of oil and transfer them to the casserole with a slotted spoon. Repeat with the remaining chicken.

4. Combine the braising liquid ingredients, and pour the mixture over the chicken and onions. Bring the liquid to a boil over medium-high heat, reduce the heat to medium low, add the mushrooms, cover the casserole, and simmer the chicken for 35 minutes.

5. Add the water chestnuts and cashew nuts, and simmer the stew for another 5 minutes. Discard the ginger slice, and add the snow peas. Stir the cornstarch and water binder together and mix it into the liquid until slightly thickened.

6. Add the sesame oil, and mix all the ingredients well. Serve the chicken hot.

Preparation time: 1 hour to soak mushrooms; 10 to 15 minutes to brown chicken
Cooking time: About 40 minutes
Serves: 4

SOY SAUCE CHICKEN

For this dish, the chicken is cooked whole. You can cut the cooked chicken into small pieces and reassemble it on a serving platter, Chinese style, or you can put the whole chicken on a platter and carve it at the dining table, Western style. It can be served hot or at room temperature.

Braising Liquid

1	cup black soy sauce
¾	cup sherry
2	teaspoons five-spice powder
2	tablespoons brown sugar
3	cloves garlic, peeled and flattened
1	slice fresh ginger root, ½-inch thick, flattened
2	cups water

Chicken

3- to 3½-pound frying chicken, cleaned and left whole

Binder and Final Seasoning

1	teaspoon cornstarch
1	teaspoon cold water
¼	teaspoon sesame oil

Instructions

1. Assemble the braising liquid ingredients in a casserole large enough (about 4 quarts) to hold the chicken. Bring the liquid to a boil over high heat. Put in the chicken, breast side down. When liquid comes back to a boil, reduce the heat to low, cover the casserole, and simmer the chicken for 1 hour, turning it several times, from side to side and from breast to back, to cook it evenly.

2. Transfer the chicken to a platter, and let it cool. Cut it into small pieces and reassemble it, or leave it whole.

3. Strain 1 cup of the braising liquid into a small saucepan. Bring the liquid to a simmer, stir in the mixed cornstarch and water binder, and cook the sauce, stirring it until it is slightly thickened. (You can freeze any remaining braising liquid to use for red-cooked dishes.)

4. Add the sesame oil, and give everything a final stir. Pour the sauce over the hot or cooled chicken, or serve it separately.

Preparation time: 5 minutes
Cooking time: 1 hour
Serves: 8 as an appetizer, 4 as a main course

LEMON CHICKEN

There are almost as many versions of Lemon Chicken as there are of sweet-and-sour sauces and of Chinese roast (or barbecued) pork. This recipe is an adaptation for casserole cooking of a version of Lemon Chicken that I used when I was a partner in a catering business.

Ingredients

Vegetable oil for browning chicken
3- to 3½-pound frying chicken, cut into small pieces (see page 36)

Braising Liquid

4   tablespoons thin soy sauce
4   tablespoons sherry
¼   teaspoon sugar
2   cloves garlic, peeled and flattened
1   slice fresh ginger root, ⅛-inch thick, flattened
¾   teaspoon sesame oil
2   whole star anise
2   dried chili peppers, broken in half (use both seeds and pods)
½   cup chicken broth

Lemon Sauce

¾   cup fresh lemon juice
¾   cup sugar
   Rind of 1 lemon, finely grated

Binder

2   teaspoons cornstarch
2   teaspoons cold water

Garnish

1   scallion, cut into ¼-inch rounds (use both green and white parts) (optional)

Instructions

1. Set a large, heavy skillet or a wok over high heat. Pour about 1½ tablespoons of oil into the pan, tilting it to coat the cooking surface with the oil. When the oil is hot, add half the chicken pieces, and brown them on all sides (about 8 minutes).

2. Meanwhile, mix the braising liquid ingredients in a 3½- or 4-quart casserole. Transfer the browned chicken to the casserole, using a slotted spoon so that any excess oil will be drained off.

3. There should be enough oil in the skillet to brown the remaining chicken; if not, add a little more (about 1 tablespoon). Brown the second batch of chicken, and transfer the pieces to the casserole.

4. Bring the braising liquid to a boil, reduce the heat to medium low, cover the casserole, and simmer the chicken for 30 to 35 minutes, or until it is done.

5. While the chicken is simmering, combine the lemon juice and sugar in a small saucepan, and cook the mixture over low heat, stirring constantly, until the sugar is dissolved. Let the sauce simmer for 10 minutes. Stir the cornstarch and water binder together, mix it into the lemon sauce, and continue to cook and stir the sauce until it thickens. Add the grated lemon rind, and give everything a final stir.

6. With a slotted spoon, transfer the chicken to a serving bowl, draining it of the braising liquid. (The braising liquid can be frozen and used again.) Pour the lemon sauce over the chicken, sprinkle it with the scallion rounds, and serve it hot.

Preparation time: 10 minutes
Cooking time: 45 minutes
Serves: 4

SPICED CHICKEN GIZZARDS AND HEARTS

In the recipes in this chapter, I have made no mention of what to do with those things that come in a bag stuffed in the cavity of the chicken. Well, you can save and freeze the necks (and the wing tips if you cut them off) to make stock, freeze the livers, and freeze the gizzards and hearts together. By accumulating these innards in separate containers in the freezer, you will eventually have enough of each to make a meal. With an assortment of vegetables, they make an economical one-dish meal.

Ingredients

    Vegetable oil for browning gizzards, hearts, and onions
1   pound chicken gizzards and hearts, trimmed of any fat, gizzards cut in half
1   medium-sized onion, cut in half from top to bottom, peeled and cut in ¼-inch slices along the grain
2   potatoes (about ½ pound), peeled and cut into 1-inch cubes
2   carrots, peeled and cut into ½-inch diagonal slices
2   ribs celery, cut into ½-inch diagonal slices

Sauce

¼   cup sherry
¼   teaspoon sugar
½   teaspoon five-spice powder
2   cloves garlic, peeled and mashed
1   slice fresh ginger root, ⅛-inch thick, flattened
    8-ounce can tomato sauce

Final Seasoning

½ teaspoon sesame oil

Instructions

1. Put a large frying pan or a wok over high heat, and add about 1½ tablespoons of oil, tilting the pan to coat the cooking surface. When the oil is hot, add the chicken gizzards, hearts, and onions, and cook them, stirring, until the onions are translucent.

2. Mix the sauce ingredients in a 2½-quart casserole. Add the gizzards, hearts, onions, potatoes, carrots, and celery, and mix all the ingredients well.

3. Bring the sauce to a boil, reduce the heat to medium low, cover the casserole, and simmer the stew for 1½ hours, stirring it occasionally. Then discard the slice of ginger. The stew will be thick enough not to need a cornstarch and water binder.

4. Stir in the sesame oil, and serve the stew hot.

Preparation time: 20 minutes
Cooking time: 1½ hours
Serves: 6 as part of a Chinese meal

SWEET-AND-SOUR CHICKEN

This recipe is a variation of the recipe for Lemon Chicken. The difference is in the sauce.

Ingredients

Vegetable oil for browning chicken
3- to 3½-pound frying chicken, cut into small pieces (see page 36)

Braising Liquid

4 tablespoons thin soy sauce
4 tablespoons sherry
¼ teaspoon sugar
2 cloves garlic, peeled and flattened
1 slice fresh ginger root, ⅛-inch thick, flattened
¾ teaspoon sesame oil
2 whole star anise
2 dried chili peppers, broken in half (use both seeds and pods)
½ cup chicken broth

Sweet-and-Sour Sauce

½ cup cider vinegar
½ cup sugar
¼ cup orange juice
¼ cup pineapple juice
3 tablespoons tomato catsup
½ teaspoon salt

Binder

2½ teaspoons cornstarch
2½ teaspoons cold water

Instructions

1. Set a large, heavy skillet or a wok over high heat. Pour about 1 tablespoon of oil into the pan, tilting it to coat the cooking surface with the oil. When the oil is hot, add half the chicken pieces, and brown them on all sides (about 8 minutes).

2. Meanwhile, mix the braising liquid ingredients in a 3½- or 4-quart casserole. Transfer the browned chicken to the casserole, using a slotted spoon so that any excess oil will be drained off.

3. There should be enough oil in the skillet to brown the remaining chicken; if not, add about 1 tablespoon. Brown the second batch of chicken, and transfer the pieces to the casserole.

4. Bring the braising liquid to a boil, reduce the heat to medium low, cover the casserole, and simmer the chicken for 30 to 35 minutes, or until it is done.

5. While the chicken is simmering, combine the sauce ingredients in a small saucepan, and cook them over low heat until sugar dissolves. Simmer the sauce, stirring occasionally, for 15 minutes.

6. Add the cornstarch and water binder to the sweet-and-sour sauce, and cook the sauce for a few minutes, stirring until it has thickened smoothly. Transfer the chicken to a serving platter with a slotted spoon to drain it of any braising liquid. (You can freeze this sauce to use in red-cooked dishes.) Pour the sweet-and-sour sauce over the chicken and serve hot.

Preparation time: 10 minutes
Cooking time: 45 minutes
Serves: 4

SHERRIED CHICKEN LIVERS WITH SHALLOTS AND MUSHROOMS

This particular dish could be Continental, but with the addition of soy sauce and sesame oil, it takes on Chinese characteristics. Add some freshly grated ginger root during the last five minutes of cooking for extra piquancy.

Ingredients

1   pound chicken livers, halved
     Vegetable oil for sautéeing shallots and mushrooms
5   shallots, peeled and cut from top to base into ⅛-inch slices
¼   pound fresh mushrooms, cut into ¼-inch slices

Braising Liquid

2   tablespoons black soy sauce
¼   cup sherry
½   teaspoon sugar
     White pepper to taste

Binder and Final Seasoning

1   teaspoon cornstarch
1   teaspoon cold water
¼   teaspoon sesame oil

Instructions

1. Bring 2 quarts of water to a boil in a 3-quart pot. Add the chicken livers, and poach them at a simmer for a few minutes, just long enough to set them, until they are slightly firm and their color changes. Drain the livers.

2. Mix the braising liquid ingredients in a 1½-quart casserole, and add the chicken livers.

3. Put a large frying pan or a wok over high heat, and pour in enough oil to coat the bottom (about 1½ tablespoons), tilting the pan to coat the cooking surface thoroughly. When the oil is hot, add the shallots and mushrooms, and cook them, stirring, over medium heat until the shallots become translucent. Add the mushrooms and shallots to the livers, and mix them well.

4. Bring the liquid to a boil, reduce the heat to medium low, cover the casserole, and simmer the chicken livers for about 20 minutes.

5. Stir the cornstarch and water binder together, and mix it into the liquid. Cook the sauce for a few minutes, until it has thickened slightly.

6. Stir in the sesame oil, and serve the chicken livers hot.

Preparation time: 15 to 20 minutes
Cooking time: 20 to 30 minutes
Serves: 4

PORK

Of all the domesticated animals, the pig has the longest history in China and has always been the principal source of meat. The pig can be penned in a small space, can be fed kitchen waste (such as rice husks and vegetable peelings), and is an economical source of high-quality protein.

The Chinese word for meat is usually used to refer to pork; other kinds of meat are identified by naming the animal first: "cow meat," "sheep meat." The Chinese character for household or home is the pictograph roof placed over the pictograph pig. Chinese villagers customarily sheltered pigs under their roofs. I remember hearing my mother and cousin describe how, during visits to relatives in small villages, they often wakened in the middle of the night by a sudden up-and-down movement of the bed. It felt as if an earthquake had struck, but actually, it was a pig trying to find a sleeping place under the bed!

It is said that in the time of Marco Polo lusty Chinese warlords preferred to eat pigs raw and would devour whole legs of uncooked pork at one sitting. The more fastidious people of that period preferred their pork baked in clay first, then simmered in a rich broth of chicken, herbs, and wine. Be assured, the recipes in this chapter call for longish periods of cooking in liquid.

I have included a number of sparerib recipes. Technically, spareribs are pork and are from the thoracic cavity, not the loin. They are often packaged by the rack (a slab of ribs from one side). Butchers use the expression three down in referring to the weight and size of the ribs, meaning one rack of ribs weighing three pounds or less. For recipes calling for ribs cut into two-inch sections, have the butcher cut them for you unless you have a very heavy meat cleaver, see page 32.

LION'S HEAD CASSEROLE

Essentially, this dish consists of meatballs (traditionally made of pork, although you can substitute beef if you wish) served on a bed of shredded Chinese cabbage. I love the way the Chinese use such fanciful names for some of their dishes: The meatballs represent the heads of lions, and the shredded cabbage, their manes.

Ingredients

1   small head Chinese cabbage (about 1½ pounds), cut crosswise into ¼-inch slices
1½ pounds boned pork loin, minced to hamburger consistency with two cleavers or a food processor
6   water chestnuts, diced into ⅛-inch cubes
2   tablespoons ham, finely minced
1   egg, lightly beaten
4   teaspoons thin soy sauce
4   teaspoons sherry
1   teaspoon sugar
½   teaspoon sesame oil
⅛   teaspoon grated fresh ginger root
¼   teaspoon white pepper
2   tablespoons cornstarch mixed with 2 teaspoons cold water
     Vegetable oil for browning meatballs

Braising Liquid

1   cup chicken broth
4   tablespoons oyster sauce

Binder and Final Seasoning

1   tablespoon cornstarch
1   tablespoon cold water
½   teaspoon sesame oil

Instructions

1. Line a 10½-inch casserole (or a heavy frying pan) with half the shredded Chinese cabbage. Reserve the rest of the cabbage.

2. In a large bowl, combine the pork, water chestnuts, ham, egg, soy sauce, sherry, sugar, sesame oil, grated ginger, pepper, and the cornstarch and water. Mix well.

3. From this mixture, shape meatballs 1¾ inches in diameter (you will have about 16), laying the finished ones on a large plate. (Because this is a rather wet mixture, the meatballs will tend to flatten out. Do not worry about that.)

4. Heat a heavy skillet over medium-high heat, and add about 1½ tablespoons of oil to the pan; tilt the pan to coat it completely with oil. When the pan is hot, place the meatballs in it, and brown them on all sides (about 8 minutes). (Depending upon the size of your pan, you may have to brown the meatballs in two or more batches.)

5. Using a pair of tongs or a slotted spoon, carefully transfer the browned meatballs to the cabbage-lined casserole. Sprinkle the remaining cabbage on top of the meatballs.

6. Combine the chicken broth and oyster sauce, and pour the mixture over the cabbage and meatballs.

7. Set the casserole over high heat, and bring the sauce to a boil. Immediately turn the heat to low or medium low, cover the casserole, and simmer the lions' heads for 45 minutes.

8. Stir the cornstarch and water together to make a binder, and mix it into the sauce. Cover the casserole, and simmer its contents for a few minutes until the sauce has thickened.

9. Stir in the sesame oil, and serve the casserole hot.

Preparation time: 20 to 25 minutes
Cooking time: 55 to 60 minutes
Serves: 3 or 4 as a main course, 6 to 8 as part of a Chinese meal

CURRIED PORK STEW

Cuban-Chinese restaurants have proliferated in the New York City area. Most of them have a set menu but feature daily specials. Inevitably, one is a pork stew. This version includes a little curry to vary the taste.

Ingredients

  Vegetable oil for browning pork and onions
2 pounds boned pork loin, cut into 1½-inch cubes
1 large onion, cut in half from top to bottom, peeled, and cut into ¼-inch slices along the grain
4 carrots, peeled and cut into ½-inch chunks
3 ribs celery, cut into ½-inch lengths
2 medium-sized potatoes, peeled and cut into 1-inch cubes
1 green pepper, stemmed, seeded, and cut into 1-inch squares

Braising Liquid

¼ cup black soy sauce
¼ cup sherry
1 teaspoon sugar
2½ tablespoons curry powder (or to taste)
½ teaspoon chili powder (or to taste)
  8-ounce can tomato sauce
¾ cup chicken broth
2 cloves garlic, peeled and flattened

Binder and Final Seasoning

2 teaspoons cornstarch
2 teaspoons cold water
½ teaspoon sesame oil

Instructions

1. Put a large frying pan or wok over high heat, and put about 1½ tablespoons of oil into it; swirl the oil to coat the inside of the pan. When the oil is hot, add the pork cubes and onions. Brown the pork on all sides, turning it frequently.

2. Transfer the browned pork and onions to a 3-quart casserole, using a slotted spoon to drain any excess oil. Combine the meat and onions with the carrots, celery, potatoes, and green pepper.

3. Mix the ingredients for the braising liquid, and pour the liquid into the casserole. Stir everything well.

4. Bring the braising liquid to a boil over high heat. Reduce the heat to medium low, cover the casserole, and simmer the stew for 1 hour.

5. Prepare the cornstarch and water binder, and mix it into the stew.

6. Drizzle the sesame oil over the stew, give it a final stir, and serve it at once.

Preparation time: 15 minutes
Cooking time: 1 hour
Serves: 6

OYSTER SAUCE PORK WITH GREEN BEANS AND CELLOPHANE NOODLES

The cellophane noodles absorb the sauce and thicken the consistency of this dish, making a binder unnecessary.

Ingredients

2   packages (2 ounces each) cellophane noodles
    Salt for browning pork
2   pounds boned pork loin, cut into 1½-inch cubes
½   pound green beans, trimmed and cut into 2-inch pieces

Braising Liquid

3   tablespoons thin soy sauce
¼   cup oyster sauce
¼   cup sherry
¼   teaspoon sugar
2   cloves garlic, peeled and flattened
1   slice fresh ginger root, ⅛-inch thick, flattened
1   cup chicken broth

Final Seasoning

½   teaspoon sesame oil

Instructions

1. Soak the cellophane noodles in plenty of warm water for 30 minutes.

2. Meanwhile, put a large frying pan or a wok over high heat. Sprinkle 1 teaspoon of salt into the pan. When the salt is hot, add the pork cubes, and brown them in their own fat (about 10 minutes), turning them from time to time.

3. Mix the braising liquid ingredients in a 3-quart casserole. When the pork cubes have browned, use a slotted spoon to transfer them to the casserole.

4. Bring the liquid to a boil over high heat. Reduce the heat to medium low, add the green beans, cover the casserole, and simmer the stew for 30 minutes. Discard the slice of ginger.

5. Drain the soaked cellophane noodles, stir them into the casserole, and cook the stew gently for another 30 minutes.

6. Stir in the sesame oil, and serve at once.

Preparation time: 30 minutes
Cooking time: 1 hour
Serves: 6

PORK AND CELLOPHANE NOODLES IN WHITE BEAN CURD CHEESE SAUCE

Here is another economical high-protein dish. White bean curd cheese is not for everyone. If you have tasted it and can't stand it, substitute oyster sauce. If you don't like oyster sauce either, don't cook this dish. With only chicken broth, soy sauce, and sherry, it is a little too much on the bland side.

The fresh coriander (Chinese parsley) leaves are too pungent for some palates. You can use plain-leaved parsley instead, if you prefer.

Marinade

1   tablespoon thin soy sauce
1   tablespoon sherry
¼   teaspoon sugar
⅛   teaspoon grated fresh ginger root
½   teaspoon sesame oil

Meat

1   pound boned pork (from chops), cut into strips 2 inches long, 1 inch wide, and ¼ inch thick

Noodles

2   packages (2 ounces each) cellophane noodles

Egg Strips

2   eggs, well beaten
    Vegetable oil for cooking omelets

Sauce

1½ cups chicken broth

2　tablespoons thin soy sauce
2　tablespoons sherry
1　teaspoon sugar
3　cakes white bean curd cheese (or 3 tablespoons oyster sauce)

Final Seasoning and Garnish

½　teaspoon sesame oil
Fresh coriander leaves, if available (optional), or parsley

Instructions

1. Mix the marinade well, and pour it over the pork strips, making sure that the meat is well coated. Marinate the pork for at least 1 hour at room temperature.

2. Soak the cellophane noodles in plenty of warm water for 30 minutes; then drain them.

3. Beat the eggs lightly, and fry them very quickly in a moderately hot frying pan, using 1 teaspoon of oil. As soon as the eggs have formed a thin omelet, flip the omelet over, and cook it for 1 or 2 minutes on the second side. Cut it into 2-by-¼-inch strips.

4. Combine all the sauce ingredients, mixing them well. (It is almost impossible to get a smooth sauce; the white bean curd cheese will break down into lumps.)

5. Put the sauce into a 1½ quart casserole. Add the drained cellophane noodles and the marinated pork, and mix well. Bring the sauce to a boil over high heat. Then reduce the heat to low, cover the casserole, and simmer for 30 minutes.

6. Drizzle the sesame oil over the noodles and pork, and give everything a final stir. Sprinkle the egg strips and coriander leaves over the top, and serve the pork and noodles hot.

Preparation time: 1¼ hours
Cooking time: 30 to 35 minutes
Serves: 2 to 3

LICHEE PORK

Pork is a meat that goes very well with fruit. It is especially wonderful with lichees in this slightly spicy casserole.

Ingredients

Salt for browning pork
2 pounds boned pork loin, cut into 1- to 1½-inch cubes

Braising Liquid

¼ cup black soy sauce
¼ cup sherry
½ cup reserved lichee syrup
1 star anise
1 dried chili pepper, broken in half (use seeds and pod)
2 cloves garlic, peeled and flattened
1 slice fresh ginger root, ⅛-inch thick, flattened

Fruit

20-ounce can lichee fruit, drained (reserve syrup)

Binder and Final Seasoning

2 teaspoons cornstarch
2 teaspoons cold water
½ teaspoon sesame oil

Instructions

1. Heat a large, heavy skillet or a wok over high heat, and sprinkle 1 teaspoon of salt into it. When the salt is hot, add the pork cubes, which will start to brown in their own fat. Brown the cubes on all sides (about 10 minutes), stirring and turning them occasionally.

2. Meanwhile, mix all the braising liquid ingredients in a casserole large enough (3 quarts or larger) to hold the pork and the lichees. Bring the liquid to a boil, reduce the heat to medium low, and add the browned pork cubes. Cover the casserole, and simmer the meat for 45 minutes.

3. Add the lichees, and simmer the stew another 10 minutes. Discard the slice of ginger.

4. Stir the cornstarch and water to make a binder, and mix it into the simmering liquid. Cook the sauce for a few minutes until it has thickened smoothly.

5. Drizzle the sesame oil over the pork and fruit, and give all the ingredients a final stir. Serve the pork hot.

Preparation time: 15 minutes
Cooking time: 1 hour
Serves: 4 as a main course, 8 as part of a Chinese meal

MINCED PORK AND VEGETABLES WITH BLACK BEAN AND GARLIC SAUCE

Salted black beans and garlic together make one of the unique sauces used in Chinese cooking. There is nothing remotely resembling this flavoring in Western cooking. It is the principal seasoning for lobster, crab, or clams Cantonese, yet it can also be used with various meats with equal success.

Marinade

4　teaspoons thin soy sauce
4　teaspoons sherry
½　teaspoon sugar
¼　teaspoon sesame oil

Meat and Vegetables

1　pound minced pork
4　dried black Oriental mushrooms
　　Vegetable oil for browning pork
4　teaspoons salted black beans, rinsed, drained, and mashed
3　cloves garlic, peeled and very finely minced
1　cup frozen peas, thawed
½　cup water chestnuts, cut into ¼-inch dice
¼　cup bamboo shoots, cut into ¼-inch dice

Braising Liquid

1　teaspoon thin soy sauce
1　tablespoon sherry
½　teaspoon sugar
½　cup chicken broth

Binder and Final Seasonings

1　teaspoon cornstarch

1   teaspoon cold water
½   teaspoon sesame oil
2   scallions, trimmed and cut into ¼-inch rounds (use both green and white parts)

Instructions

1. Mix the marinade, and mix it again with the minced pork. Let the pork marinate at room temperature for 1 hour.

2. At the same time, cover the dried mushrooms with warm water, and let them soak 1 hour. Drain mushrooms, trim off the stems, and cut the mushrooms into ¼-inch dice.

3. Put a large frying pan or a wok over medium-high heat, and add just enough oil (about 1½ tablespoons) to coat the pan, tilting the pan to cover the cooking surface thoroughly. When the oil is hot, add the marinated pork, black beans, and garlic. Cook them, stirring, until the pork has browned. Add diced mushrooms, peas, water chestnuts, and bamboo shoots. Mix everything well, and remove the pan from heat.

4. Mix the braising liquid in a 1½-or 2-quart casserole, and add the meat and vegetables. Blend well. Bring ingredients to a boil, then reduce the heat to medium low, cover the casserole, and simmer the contents for 25 minutes.

5. Stir the cornstarch and water binder, and blend it into the braising liquid. Cook until slightly thickened.

6. Add the sesame oil and scallions to the casserole, give all the ingredients a final toss, and serve the stew hot.

Preparation time: 1 hour
Cooking time: 30 minutes
Serves: 4

Note: You can turn this dish into a tempting, unusual appetizer. Place a heaping spoonful of the cooked meat and vegetable mixture on the center of a lettuce leaf. Roll the leaf up, and serve the tidbit at once.

BEAN CURD CUBES STUFFED WITH MINCED PORK AND HAM

This good, inexpensive, meat-stretching dish is high in protein, as well as delicious.

Ingredients

4 squares bean curd, each cut into 4 pieces about 1½ inches square.
3 ounces minced pork (about 1 thick pork chop's worth)
2 water chestnuts, cut into ⅛-inch dice
1 tablespoon minced ham
¼ teaspoon finely chopped Chinese parsley (or scallions; use both green and white parts)

Seasonings

1 teaspoon thin soy sauce
1 teaspoon sherry
  Pinch of sugar
⅛ teaspoon sesame oil
  Pinch of white pepper

Braising Liquid

¾ cup chicken broth mixed with 2 tablespoons oyster sauce (see step 5)

Binder

½ teaspoon cornstarch
½ teaspoon cold water

Garnish

1 scallion (optional), cut into ¼-inch rounds (use both green and white parts)

Instructions

1. Using a melon ball cutter or the tip of a teaspoon, scoop out a hollow in the top of each bean curd square.

2. Mix the minced pork, water chestnuts, ham, and Chinese parsley (or scallions) with the seasonings, which you have first mixed together.

3. Pack a portion of the mixture into each scooped-out bean curd, mounding it up slightly.

4. Place the bean curd squares in a shallow casserole large enough (about 12 inches in diameter) to hold the 16 squares in a single layer.

5. Mix the braising liquid, and pour it over the squares. Set the casserole over high heat, and bring the liquid to a boil. Immediately reduce the heat to the lowest setting, cover the casserole, and simmer the stuffed bean curd squares for 15 to 20 minutes. (If the liquid evaporates too fast, add another ½ cup chicken broth mixed with 1 tablespoon oyster sauce. However, if the casserole lid fits tightly, this probably will not be necessary.)

6. Transfer the bean curd squares with a slotted spatula to a serving platter. Mix the cornstarch and water binder, and add it to the liquid. Stir the sauce over medium heat until slightly thickened. Pour the sauce over the stuffed bean curd squares.

7. Garnish the dish, if you like, with the scallion rounds, and serve it hot.

Preparation time: 20 minutes
Cooking time: 35 to 40 minutes
Serves: 2 as a main course, 4 or more as an appetizer

CELLOPHANE NOODLES WITH EGG THREADS AND CHINESE SAUSAGE

"Powdered silk" is the literal translation of the Cantonese name of the Chinese ingredient commonly referred to as <u>cellophane noodles</u> or <u>shiny noodles</u>. These are not noodles in the Western sense of being made of flour, water, and eggs; they are actually made from the starch of mung beans and are nutritious and very inexpensive. Here is a way of making a tasty and unusual dish that dazzles the mind with its simplicity and purity of taste. This is a very Chinese family-style dish. It is also economical. What more could you ask?

Ingredients

	2-ounce package cellophane noodles
2	Chinese sausages
	Vegetable oil for cooking egg threads
1	egg, lightly beaten
1	scallion, cut in 2-inch pieces, then sliced lengthwise into ⅛-inch slivers

Braising Liquid

1	tablespoon thin soy sauce
2	tablespoons sherry
1	tablespoon oyster sauce
¼	teaspoon sugar
1	cup chicken broth (see step 5)

Final Seasoning

¼	teaspoon sesame oil

Instructions

1. Cover the cellophane noodles with water, and soak them for 30 minutes.

2. Meanwhile, steam the Chinese sausages (if you have no steamer, put the sausages in a colander over hot water) until heated through (10 to 15 minutes). Cut the sausages into ¼-inch diagonal slices.

3. Heat 1½ tablespoons of oil in a 6-inch (or larger) frying pan, and cook the egg very quickly. When it has formed a barely firm thin omelet, turn it, and cook the second side for 1 or 2 minutes. Cut the omelet into threads ¼ inch wide.

4. Drain the softened cellophane noodles. Combine the noodles and the Chinese sausage slices in a heavy 1½- or 2-quart casserole.

5. Mix the braising liquid ingredients, and pour the mixture into the casserole. Bring the liquid to a boil over high heat. Then reduce the heat to medium low, and simmer the casserole for 20 minutes. (If the noodles begin to dry out, add about ¼ cup more chicken broth.)

6. Mix the egg threads into the cellophane noodles and sausages. Cover the casserole, and simmer the contents for 3 to 5 minutes until the sausages and egg threads are heated through.

7. Drizzle the sesame oil over the ingredients, give everything a final stir, and serve the casserole hot. Garnish with the scallion slivers.

Preparation time: 30 minutes
Cooking time: 30 minutes
Serves: 2

BRAISED PORK LOIN WITH TURNIPS

Because pork must be cooked thoroughly, there is a tendency to overcook it. That is why pork roasted in the oven usually comes out dry and stringy. But if you cook a pork loin with a small amount of soy sauce and sherry in a covered pot over a low fire on top of the stove, you will have a tender, moist, and flavorful dish.

Ingredients

4   large lettuce leaves (or enough to line a
     3½-quart casserole)
1   large onion, cut in half from top to bottom, peeled, and cut
     into ¼-inch slices along the grain
     5-rib pork loin roast (about 3½ pounds)
2   cloves garlic, peeled and cut into slivers
     Vegetable oil for browning pork
3   turnips (about 1½ pounds), peeled and cut into 8 sections
     each

Braising Liquid

¼   cup black soy sauce
¼   cup sherry
1   teaspoon sugar
½   cup chicken broth

Binder and Final Seasoning

1   tablespoon cornstarch
1   tablespoon cold water
½   teaspoon sesame oil

Instructions

1. Line a 3½-quart casserole with the lettuce leaves (see page 25). Scatter the onion slices over the lettuce leaves.

2. Make small slashes over the entire surface of the pork roast, and insert the slivers of garlic into them.

3. Heat about 1½ tablespoons of oil in a large frying pan or a wok, tilting the pan to coat the entire cooking surface, and brown the roast on all sides. Place pork, bone side down, on the bed of lettuce and onions in the casserole.

4. Brown the turnip sections in the same pan in which you browned the pork. Place them in the casserole around the pork.

5. Stir the braising liquid ingredients together until the sugar is dissolved, and pour the liquid over the pork and turnips. Bring the liquid to a boil over high heat; then reduce the heat to medium low, cover the casserole, and simmer the ingredients for 3½ hours, turning the pork from time to time.

6. When the pork is done, transfer it to a serving platter, and surround it with the lettuce, onions, and turnips. (To test for doneness, make a cut in the center next to the bone. If juices are clear, not pink, the pork is done. Or check with a meat thermometer in the thickest part of the meat; it should read 170° to 175°F.)

7. Mix the cornstarch and water together, and stir the binder into the braising liquid.

8. Stir in the sesame oil; then simmer the sauce for another 5 minutes. Either pour the sauce over the meat, or serve it separately. Serve the pork loin hot.

Preparation time: 5 to 10 minutes
Cooking time: 3½ hours
Serves: 6

SPICY TWICE-COOKED PORK CHOPS WITH WATERCRESS

This is a variation on the restaurant dish called Twice-cooked Pork, in which the meat is first simmered, then sliced and stir-fried. For casserole cooking, I have reversed that process and embellished the dish with watercress. This is a tasty way of preparing pork chops so that they won't come out dry and stringy.

Braising Liquid

3   tablespoons thin soy sauce
3   tablespoons sherry
½   teaspoon sugar
2   cloves garlic, peeled and flattened
1   slice fresh ginger root, ⅛-inch thick, flattened
2   tablespoons hoisin sauce
1   tablespoon ground brown bean sauce
2   dried chili peppers, broken in half (use both seeds and pods)
1   tablespoon vinegar (rice, white, or cider)
1   cup chicken broth

Other Ingredients

Vegetable oil for browning onions and pork
1   large onion, cut in half from top to bottom, peeled, and cut into ¼-inch slices along the grain
4   pork chops, each roughly ¾ inch thick, trimmed of excess fat
1   bunch watercress, washed, drained, and any thick stems removed

Binder and Final Seasoning

4   teaspoons cornstarch
4   teaspoons cold water
¼   teaspoon sesame oil

Instructions

1. Assemble the braising liquid ingredients in a casserole large enough (10 inches in diameter) to hold the pork chops in 1 or 2 layers.

2. Put a large frying pan or a wok over high heat, and add enough oil to coat the pan (about 1½ tablespoons), tilting the pan to cover the entire cooking surface. When the oil is hot, add the onions, and fry them, stirring, until they are translucent. Use a slotted spoon to transfer the fried onions to the casserole; arrange them so that they make a bed for the pork chops.

3. Add 1 tablespoon of oil to the frying pan, and when it is hot, brown the pork chops on both sides. Transfer them to the casserole, using a slotted spoon to drain them of excess oil; arrange them in 1 or 2 layers on the bed of onions.

4. Bring the liquid in the casserole to a boil over high heat; then reduce the heat to medium low, cover the casserole, and simmer the pork chops for 45 minutes, turning them once.

5. Skim off any excess fat. Discard the ginger slice. Stir together the cornstarch and water binder, and mix it into the sauce.

6. Stir in the sesame oil, lay the watercress on top of the pork chops, cover the casserole, and simmer everything for another 5 minutes. Serve the pork chops hot.

Preparation time: 10 minutes
Cooking time: 45 to 60 minutes
Serves: 4

CHINESE-STYLE SPARERIBS AND SAUERKRAUT

Most cultures have some way of preserving vegetables either by salting or by pickling them in a vinegar-brine solution. The Chinese pickle many kinds of vegetables, including various members of the cabbage family, which resemble the familiar sauerkraut. Without the seasonings that make it Chinese, this recipe might be identified with Germany, Alsace, or Poland.

Ingredients

Salt for browning spareribs
3 to 3½ pounds spareribs, trimmed of surplus fat and cut into 4-rib slabs

Braising Liquid

½ cup black soy sauce
½ cup sherry
3 tablespoons brown sugar
¼ cup cider vinegar
2 whole star anise
1 dried chili pepper, broken in half (use both seeds and pod)
2 cloves garlic, peeled and flattened
1 slice fresh ginger root, ⅛-inch thick, flattened

Sauerkraut

2 pounds sauerkraut (preferably the fresh kind packed in plastic bags)

Binder and Final Seasoning

1 tablespoon cornstarch
1 tablespoon cold water
½ teaspoon sesame oil

Instructions

1. Put a large frying pan or a wok over high heat, and sprinkle about 1 teaspoon of salt into it. When the salt is hot, put into it as many slabs of spareribs as will fit and brown them, turning them as necessary (about 10 minutes). (You will probably have to do the ribs in two or three batches.)

2. Meanwhile, assemble the braising liquid ingredients in a large casserole (about 4 quarts). Place the spareribs in the casserole as each batch is browned, and mix them with the liquid. Bring the liquid to a boil over high heat; then reduce the heat to low or medium low, cover the casserole, and simmer the ribs for 40 minutes, switching them from top to bottom once.

3. Rinse the sauerkraut in cold water, and drain it. Place it on top of the spareribs, and cook the ribs and sauerkraut for 15 minutes. Discard the slice of ginger.

4. Stir the cornstarch and water together, and mix the binder into the braising liquid. Simmer the ingredients for another 5 minutes.

5. Sprinkle the sesame oil over the ribs and sauerkraut, give everything a final stir, and serve the casserole hot.

Preparation time: 20 minutes
Cooking time: 1 hour
Serves: 4 or 5

SPARERIBS IN BLACK BEAN, GARLIC, AND EGG SAUCE

This hearty dish makes a splendid cold-weather meal. The black bean, garlic, and egg sauce goes especially well with hot white rice. You might also want to serve a Chinese-style green vegetable or a green vegetable cooked American style.

Ingredients

Salt for browning spareribs
3   pounds (about 1 rack) spareribs, separated, trimmed of surplus fat, and cut into 2-inch lengths (see page 32)
3   tablespoons salted black beans, rinsed, drained, and mashed
4   cloves garlic, peeled and finely minced

Braising Liquid

1½ tablespoons thin soy sauce
3   tablespoons sherry
½   teaspoon sugar
1   slice fresh ginger root, ⅛-inch thick, flattened
½   cup water

Binder and Final Seasoning

4   teaspoons cornstarch
4   teaspoons cold water
2   eggs, lightly beaten
½   teaspoon sesame oil

Instructions

1. Put a large frying pan or a wok over high heat, and sprinkle about 1 teaspoon salt into the pan. When the salt is hot, brown half the spareribs (about 10 minutes). The ribs will start to brown in their own fat; turn them occasionally.

2. While the ribs are browning, combine the braising liquid ingredients in a 3-quart casserole.

3. When the first batch of ribs is browned, transfer them to the casserole. Brown the remaining ribs (about 10 minutes). Add the mashed black beans and the garlic to the second batch of browning spareribs.

4. With a slotted spoon, transfer the second batch of browned spareribs and the seasoning from the frying pan to the casserole, leaving behind any fat. Bring the liquid in the casserole to a boil over high heat, reduce the heat to medium low, cover the casserole, and simmer the spareribs for 1 hour, turning them once or twice. Discard the slice of ginger.

5. Stir the cornstarch and water binder together, and mix it into the braising liquid over low heat. When the sauce has thickened add the lightly beaten eggs. Stir the sauce well until the egg has coagulated.

6. Drizzle the sesame oil into the casserole, and serve the spareribs hot.

Preparation time: 20 minutes
Cooking time: 1 hour
Serves: 3 or 4

CHUTNEY SPARERIBS

Here are the ubiquitous spareribs in yet another form. This dish combines five of the Eight Immortal Flavors: salty, sweet, sour, hot and fragrant. (The other three are bland, bitter, and "golden".)

Ingredients

Salt for browning spareribs
3½ to 4 pounds spareribs, trimmed of surplus fat, separated, and cut into 2-inch slices (see page 32)

Braising Liquid

3 tablespoons black soy sauce
3 tablespoons sherry
1 teaspoon sugar
½ cup water
½ cup chutney, coarsely chopped
2 tablespoons tomato catsup
3 cloves garlic, peeled and flattened
3 dried chili peppers, broken in half (use both seeds and pods)
2 whole star anise

Binder and Final Seasoning

2 teaspoons cornstarch
2 teaspoons cold water
½ teaspoon sesame oil

Instructions

1. Put a large, heavy frying pan or a wok over high heat, and sprinkle 1 teaspoon of salt into it. When the salt is hot, add half the spareribs to the pan. The ribs will begin to brown in their own fat; keep turning them to brown them on all sides (about 10 minutes).

2. Meanwhile, mix all the braising liquid ingredients in a 4-quart casserole. When the first batch of spareribs has browned, transfer the ribs to the casserole with a slotted spoon, draining them well of any fat. Brown the rest of the ribs. (There should be enough fat in the pan for this. If there isn't, add a little more salt to the bottom of the pan.)

3. Transfer the second batch of browned ribs to the casserole, draining them of any clinging fat. Mix the spareribs and the braising liquid well. Bring the liquid to a boil over high heat. Reduce the heat to low or medium low, cover the casserole, and simmer the ribs for 1 hour, turning them once or twice.

4. Stir the cornstarch and water binder, and mix it into the liquid. Cook the sauce for a few moments until it thickens.

5. Stir in the sesame oil, and simmer the ingredients a few minutes more. Serve the spareribs hot.

Preparation time: 15 to 20 minutes
Cooking time: 1 hour
Serves: 3 or 4 as a main course, 8 as an appetizer

SPARERIBS IN RED BEAN CURD CHEESE SAUCE

Spareribs cooked in this sauce are served in most Cantonese-style dumpling houses. The taste of red bean curd cheese is rather like that of white bean curd cheese.

Ingredients

Salt for browning spareribs
1   rack spareribs (about 2½ to 3 pounds), separated, trimmed of surplus fat, and cut into 2-inch lengths (see page 32)

Braising Liquid

½   square (about 2 tablespoons) red bean curd cheese
1   tablespoon thin soy sauce
2   tablespoons sherry
½   cup water
1   teaspoon sugar
2   tablespoons tomato catsup
2   cloves garlic, peeled and flattened
1   slice fresh ginger root, ⅛-inch thick, flattened

Binder

1   teaspoon cornstarch
1   teaspoon cold water

Instructions

1. Put a large frying pan or a wok over high heat, and sprinkle about 1 teaspoon of salt into it. When the salt is hot, add the spareribs. The ribs will brown in their own fat (about 10 minutes); turn them occasionally. (You may have to do this in two batches.)

2. Combine the braising liquid ingredients in a 3-quart casserole. Use a slotted spoon to transfer the spareribs to the casserole, draining them of any fat. Stir the ribs around so that they are well coated with liquid.

3. Bring the liquid to a boil over high heat. Reduce the heat to medium low, cover the casserole, and simmer the spareribs for 1 hour, turning them occasionally. Discard the slice of ginger.

4. Mix the cornstarch and water binder, and stir it into the braising liquid. Simmer the sauce until it has thickened lightly. Serve the spareribs hot.

Preparation time: 20 minutes
Cooking time: 1 hour
Serves: 2 to 4

SPARERIBS WITH CURRIED TOMATO SAUCE

This very simple sparerib dish uses ingredients found in any supermarket: a can of tomato sauce and some curry powder. It can be made in advance and reheated.

Ingredients

Salt for browning spareribs
1 rack (about 3 pounds) of spareribs, separated and cut into 2-inch lengths (see page 32)

Braising Liquid

8-ounce can tomato sauce
2 tablespoons curry powder (or to taste)

Instructions

1. Heat a large, heavy cast-iron skillet or a wok, then sprinkle about 1 teaspoon of salt into it. When the salt is heated, add half of the spareribs, spreading them out on the cooking surface. Cook the ribs over high heat, turning them occasionally until they are browned (about 10 minutes).

2. Transfer the browned ribs to a 3-quart casserole, using a slotted spoon to drain them of any fat. Brown the remaining ribs.

3. Combine the tomato sauce and curry powder, add the mixture to the spareribs and stir well. Cover the casserole, and bring the sauce to a boil. Reduce the heat to medium low, cover the casserole, and simmer the meat for 1 hour, turning the ribs from time to time. When the ribs are tender, serve them hot.

Preparation time: 20 minutes
Cooking time: 1 hour
Serves: 3 or 4

HOME-STYLE SWEET-AND-SOUR SPARERIBS

Many Americans' first experience with Chinese food is the ubiquitous Sweet-and-Sour Spareribs, which have a very thick sauce studded with either pineapple chunks or maraschino cherries, or both. I have an aversion to maraschino cherries because I used to work in a fruit cannery in San Jose, where my job was to put three maraschino cherries in each can of fruit cocktail. When the sample room found from zero to eighteen cherries per can, they transferred me to the dicer, which was the equivalent of being sent to Siberia. The following recipe is based on the very simple way my mother used to cook sweet-and-sour spareribs. She would add pineapple only if we were going to have company. You can make this dish with or without fruit, as you wish.

Ingredients

    Salt for browning spareribs
1   rack (about 3 pounds) spareribs, separated, trimmed of excess fat, and cut into 2-inch lengths (see page 32)

Braising Liquid

3   tablespoons black soy sauce
3   tablespoons sherry
¼   cup (packed) brown sugar
⅓   cup cider vinegar
2   cloves garlic, peeled and flattened
1   slice fresh ginger root, ⅛-inch thick, flattened
½   cup water (or reserved pineapple juice if you are including fruit)
1   or 2 dried chili peppers, broken in half (use both seeds and pods if you want a little more bite to the sauce) (optional)

Fruit

1   cup canned pineapple chunks

Binder and Final Seasoning

2   teaspoons cornstarch
2   teaspoons cold water
½   teaspoon sesame oil

Instructions

1   Put a large, heavy frying pan or a wok over high heat. Sprinkle about 1 teaspoon of salt into it. When the salt is hot, add half the spareribs. Brown the ribs on all sides in their own fat (about 10 minutes). Stir the ribs around so that they do not burn.

2. Meanwhile, assemble the braising liquid ingredients in a 3-quart casserole (or any casserole large enough to hold all the ribs). Transfer the browned spareribs to the casserole, using a slotted spoon to drain them of excess fat. Brown the second batch of spareribs.

3. Bring the contents of the casserole to a boil over high heat. Reduce the heat to medium low or low, cover the casserole, and simmer the ribs for 1 hour, turning them over once or twice. If you are including the pineapple chunks, add them during the last 5 minutes of cooking. Discard the ginger slice. For more pungency, add cider vinegar to taste.

4. Stir the cornstarch water and binder, and mix it into the liquid. Cook for a few minutes until the sauce is thickened.

5. Stir in the sesame oil, and serve the ribs hot.

Preparation time: 20 minutes
Cooking time: 1 hour
Serves: 3 as a main course, 6 as an appetizer

CHINESE ROAST PORK (BARBECUED PORK)

A number of recipes in this book call for Chinese roast pork (also called barbecued pork). If you don't live near a Chinatown, there is no way to get it other than to make it yourself. So although barbecued pork does not fall under the category of Chinese casserole cookery, here is a recipe for it.

It is best to make big batches of this pork because you can freeze it. When you want to use the pork, thaw it out at room temperature, and use it as instructed in your recipe. It makes delicious sandwiches, too.

Marinade

1 cup hoisin sauce
½ cup tomato catsup
⅓ cup (packed) brown sugar (or white sugar)
⅓ cup thin soy sauce
⅓ cup sherry
2 or 3 cloves garlic, peeled and finely minced

Meat

4 pounds boned pork loin, cut into strips 5 inches long, 2 inches wide, and 1½ inches thick

Instructions

1. Mix the marinade ingredients, and marinate the pork strips in the mixture, refrigerated, for 3 hours.

2. Remove the lower racks from your oven, and place one rack at the highest position. Place a shallow roasting pan containing 1 inch of water on the bottom of the oven. Preheat the oven with the control set at 325° or 350°F.

3. Make S-shaped hooks of poultry lacers (very thin, short skewers). (In a pinch, you can use paper clips.) Insert one end of a hook into the top of each pork strip. Using kitchen tongs, hang the hooks from the top rack, making sure all the meat is positioned over the pan of water. (The water catches the drippings and prevents your oven from smoking. It also helps to keep the pork moist and tender.)

4. Roast the pork for 40 to 45 minutes. (To make sure the pork is cooked through, cut into the center of the thickest piece. If the juices run clear, the pork is done. If the juices are pink, cook the pork a little longer.) Be careful not to overcook the pork, because overcooking gives it a dry, tough texture.

5. Remove the meat from the oven, again using kitchen tongs, and serve. Or let the meat cool, divide it into ¼-pound portions, wrap it in plastic wrap or aluminum foil, and store it in the freezer.

Preparation time: 3 hours
Cooking time: About 45 minutes

PORK-FILLED EGG-POUCH DUMPLING CASSEROLE

Egg-pouch dumplings are usually assembled, steamed, and sauced, but they can be even more delicious when they are poached in a sauce.

You should be warned that assembling these dumplings can be the ultimate test of your patience, so if you have a low threshold of frustration, don't attempt this recipe. The most delicate part is making the little dumpling skins — actually thin omelets — and then filling them with the minced port mixture. If you have had experience with making French crêpes, you are ahead of the game because you know that the first few must often be thrown away until you have gotten the right heat and the right amount of oil in the pan for each crêpe.

The good news is that you can assemble these dumplings the day before, cover them with plastic wrap, and refrigerate them until time to cook them the next day.

The Filling

¼ pound pork, minced
1 teaspoon finely minced smoked ham
4 water chestnuts, finely diced
½ teaspoon thin soy sauce
½ teaspoon sherry
¼ teaspoon sugar
   Drizzle of sesame oil

Dumpling Skins

   Vegetable oil for cooking dumpling skins
5 eggs, beaten until thoroughly blended

Lettuce

Lettuce leaves to line casserole

Braising Liquid

1   cup chicken broth
1   tablespoon thin soy sauce
1   tablespoon sherry
1   teaspoon sugar
1   tablespoon oyster sauce

Binder and Final Seasoning

1   tablespoon cornstarch
1   tablespoon water
¼   teaspoon sesame oil

Garnish

Chopped parsley (or scallions)

Instructions

1. Combine the filling ingredients, and set the mixture aside for 20 to 30 minutes at room temperature to allow the flavors to blend.

2. Heat a crêpe pan (or a small, heavy cast-iron skillet). Then add enough oil (1 teaspoon) to coat the bottom of the pan. When the oil is hot, pour about 1 tablespoon of well-beaten egg into the center of the pan, and swirl the egg around until a thin omelet 2¼ to 3 inches in diameter forms in the center of the pan.

3. When the omelet has barely started to set, place 1 scant teaspoonful of the filling in its center. Using a spatula, immediately fold the pancake over into a crescent. Press the edge of the crescent shut with the edge of the spatula (see page 34). (The runny egg, pressure, and heat should seal this little dumpling shut.) Remove the filled dumpling to an oiled plate. Continue making and filling dumpling skins until all the pork mixture is used. At this point, the dumplings can

be cooled, then covered with plastic wrap and refrigerated until the next day.

4. Line a 1¼-quart casserole with lettuce leaves (see page 25). Arrange the dumplings on top of the leaves.

5. Combine the braising liquid ingredients in a saucepan, and heat the mixture over medium-high heat. When the sauce bubbles, mix and add the cornstarch and water binder and blend it with the liquid thoroughly. Cook the sauce for a few minutes until it thickens slightly. Pour the sauce over the dumplings.

6. Bring the casserole to a boil over high heat. Immediately reduce heat to medium low, cover the pot, and simmer the dumplings for a total of 20 minutes, stirring them carefully from bottom to top after 10 minutes. Stir in the sesame oil.

7. Garnish the dumplings with chopped parsley or scallions, and serve them hot.

Preparation time: 1 hour
Cooking time: 20 to 25 minutes
Yield: About 18 dumplings
Serves: 5 as an appetizer or 6 as part of a Chinese meal

LAMB

The same Chinese character is used for lamb, mutton, and goat.
Possibly because of the strong taste of the fat, lamb is not a
popular meat among the Chinese. It is eaten most in the
northern regions of China, and it is also used by Chinese
Moslems. Although my family is neither Moslem nor from the
north, we frequently had red-cooked lamb stews, usually made
with cuts that had a lot of gristle, such as the shanks, shoulder,
or breast. The texture of gristly meat that has been simmered for
a long time is particularly pleasing to the Chinese palate.

SPICY LAMB WITH SCALLIONS

Most restaurants featuring Peking-style food have a dish called Lamb with Scallions. This recipe is a spicy stewed version of that dish.

Ingredients

  Vegetable oil for browning lamb
1 pound boneless shoulder of lamb (use shoulder chops, boned and trimmed of fat), cut into pieces ½ inch by ½ inch by 2 inches

Braising Liquid

2 tablespoons black soy sauce
2 tablespoons sherry
1 teaspoon sugar
2 cloves garlic, peeled and flattened
1 slice fresh ginger root, ⅛-inch thick, flattened
1 whole star anise
2 dried red chili peppers, broken in half (use both seeds and pods)
1 tablespoon hoisin sauce
1 teaspoon ground brown bean sauce
¼ cup water

Binder and Final Seasonings

1 teaspoon cornstarch
1 teaspoon cold water
3 scallions, trimmed and cut into 2-inch pieces (use both green and white parts)
¼ teaspoon sesame oil

Instructions

1. Put a frying pan or a wok over a high flame, and pour in enough oil to coat the pan (about 1½ tablespoons), tilting the pan to make sure the entire cooking surface is covered. When the oil is hot, add the lamb, and cook the pieces, turning them, until they are a crusty brown on all sides.

2. Mix the braising liquid ingredients in a 1½-quart casserole until well blended. Transfer the lamb to the casserole, and stir until the meat is well coated with the liquid.

3. Bring the liquid to a boil over high heat. Reduce the heat to medium low, cover the casserole, and simmer the stew for about 1½ hours, or until lamb is done. Discard the slice of ginger.

4. Mix the cornstarch and water together, and blend the binder into the braising liquid. Cook the sauce for a few minutes until it thickens.

5. Stir in the scallions and sesame oil, and serve the casserole hot.

Preparation time: 10 minutes
Cooking time: About 1½ hours
Serves: 3 or 4

BRAISED LAMB WITH WHITE BEANS

This robust dish is a meal in itself, perfect for a cold winter's night. However, if you wish to try the recipe, and it doesn't happen to be a cold winter's night, please go ahead anyway.

Ingredients

½ pound (1 cup) white beans
1 bay leaf
   Salt for browning lamb and onions
3 pounds breast of lamb, trimmed of fat and cut into 2-inch pieces
1 large onion, cut in half from top to bottom, peeled, and cut into ¼-inch slices along the grain

Braising Liquid

¼ cup black soy sauce
1 cup sherry
2 cups beef broth (if broth is salty, use 1 cup broth, and add 1 cup water)
2 cloves garlic, peeled and flattened
3 ounces (½ can) tomato paste
2 whole star anise

Vegetables

4 carrots, peeled and sliced into 1½-inch chunks
3 ribs celery, cut into 1-inch pieces

Instructions

1. Cover white beans with water, refrigerate, and soak them for 24 hours at room temperature. Drain and rinse the beans, and put them into a pot with 4 cups of fresh water. Add the bay leaf, and simmer the beans, uncovered, for 1 hour, or until half cooked. (The beans will finish cooking with the lamb.) You will have about 2 cups of beans at this point.

2. Put a large, heavy frying pan or a wok over high heat, and sprinkle 1 teaspoon of salt into it. When the salt is hot, add the lamb. (Depending upon the size of your pan, you may have to brown the lamb in two batches.) The lamb will start to brown in its own fat. Add the onion, and cook the ingredients, turning them occasionally, until browned.

3. Meanwhile, mix the braising liquid ingredients in a 4-quart casserole. Transfer the browned lamb and onions to the casserole, using a slotted spoon to drain them of any fat.

4. Bring the sauce to a boil over high heat. Reduce the heat to medium low, cover the casserole, and simmer the lamb for 1 hour. Add the carrots, celery, and white beans to the pot, and mix everything well. Simmer all the ingredients for another 1½ hours, or until meat, beans, and vegetables are done. Serve the casserole hot.

Preparation time: 24 hours to soak beans;
15 minutes to cut vegetables and meat
Cooking time: 3½ hours
Serves: 6

SWEET-AND-SOUR BREAST OF LAMB

Breast of lamb, which has more ribs than meat, is an economy cut. When braised in a sweet-and-sour sauce, it makes a wonderful tidbit to serve before dinner. You can also serve it as part of a Chinese meal, in which a number of dishes are served, or even as the main course in a Western-style meal.

Ingredients

Salt for browning lamb
2½ pounds breast of lamb, trimmed of fat and cut into 2-inch chunks

Braising Liquid

2   tablespoons black soy sauce
2   tablespoons sherry
4   tablespoons brown sugar
2   cloves garlic, peeled and flattened
1   slice fresh ginger root, ⅛-inch thick, flattened
⅓   cup cider vinegar
¼   cup water

Binder and Final Seasoning

1   teaspoon cornstarch
1   teaspoon cold water
½   teaspoon sesame oil

Instructions

1. Heat a large frying pan or a wok over high flame. Sprinkle about 1 teaspoon of salt into the hot pan. When the salt is hot, add the lamb chunks. Stir lamb around. When some fat starts oozing from the meat, reduce the heat to medium high, and brown the lamb in its own fat, turning the pieces occasionally (about 10 to 15 minutes).

2. Meanwhile assemble the braising liquid ingredients in a casserole large enough (3 quarts) to hold the lamb.

3. Using a slotted spoon, transfer the browned lamb to the casserole, draining it well of excess oil. Discard the lamb fat in the pan. If there are any browned bits clinging to the pan, add ¼ cup water, set it over the heat, and scrape up the bits; then add this liquid to the casserole. (This is called deglazing the pan. It is also a good way of getting the pan almost clean.)

4. Bring the braising liquid to a boil over high heat. Adjust heat to low, cover the casserole, and simmer the lamb for 1 hour, turning the pieces once or twice. Discard the ginger slice.

5. Mix the cornstarch and water together, and stir the binder into the braising liquid. Cook the sauce for a few minutes to thicken it slightly. For more pungency, add cider vinegar to taste.

6. Mix in the sesame oil, and give all the ingredients a final stir. Serve the lamb hot.

Preparation time: 20 minutes
Cooking time: 1 hour
Serves: 2 or 3 as a main course, 6 as an appetizer, 4 as part of a Chinese meal

LAMB SHANKS WITH PLUM SAUCE

The lamb shank is a tough piece of meat made up of several muscles that taper off into tendons which, in turn, are attached to the bone and wrapped around with ligaments. There is so much connective tissue to this cut that it needs to cook a long time to make the meat tender. The connective tissue breaks down into a gelatinous texture that the Chinese like.

If you have the butcher crack the shank bone in the center, you will get an added bonus: some marrow.

Ingredients

Salt for browning lamb
4 lamb shanks (¾ to 1 pound each), trimmed of excess fat

Braising Liquid

6 tablespoons black soy sauce
6 tablespoons sherry
½ teaspoon sugar
1½ cups water
¾ cup plum sauce, with the fruits coarsely chopped (or use chutney)
3 cloves garlic, peeled and flattened
2 dried chili peppers, broken in half (use both seeds and pods)
2 whole star anise
1 slice ginger root, ¼-inch thick, flattened

Binder and Final Seasoning

1 tablespoon cornstarch
1 tablespoon cold water
½ teaspoon sesame oil

Instructions

1. Put a large frying pan or a wok over high heat, and sprinkle in about 1 teaspoon of salt. When the salt is hot, add the lamb shanks, and brown them on all sides (about 10 minutes).

2. Mix the braising liquid ingredients in a 4-quart casserole. Add the lamb shanks, and bring the liquid to a boil over high heat. Reduce the heat to medium low, cover the casserole, and simmer the shanks for 3½ to 4 hours, or until the meat is tender. Turn the lamb shanks from time to time.

3. Remove the lamb shanks to a serving dish. Skim the fat from the braising liquid, and discard the slice of ginger. Mix the cornstarch and water binder, and stir it into the liquid. Cook the sauce for a few minutes to thicken it.

4. Stir in the sesame oil, pour the sauce over the lamb shanks, and serve them hot.

Preparation time: 15 minutes
Cooking time: 3½ to 4 hours
Serves: 4

LAMB AND BEAN CURD STICKS WITH BLACK BEAN AND GARLIC SAUCE

Bean curd sticks are usually used in soups, but there is no reason why they can't be incorporated into meat dishes. The blandness of the bean curd stick goes very well with the robustness of the black bean and garlic sauce. This combination is a good way of making inexpensive, high-protein food tasty.

Ingredients

4   bean curd sticks (8 lengths), drained
    Salt for browning lamb
3   pounds lamb stew meat (breast or neck), trimmed of fat and cut into 1½-inch chunks
1   large onion, cut in half from top to bottom, peeled, and cut into ¼-inch slices along the grain
3   tablespoons salted black beans, rinsed and well mashed in a mortar
3   cloves garlic, peeled and minced

Braising Liquid

¼   cup black soy sauce
¼   cup sherry
¼   teaspoon sugar
1   slice fresh ginger root, ¼-inch thick, flattened
½   cup water

Binder and Final Seasoning

2   teaspoons cornstarch
2   teaspoons cold water
½   teaspoon sesame oil

Garnish

Fresh coriander leaves (or thinly cut scallion rounds)

Instructions

1. Soak the bean curd stick in warm water to cover for 2 hours.

2. Put a large skillet or a wok over high heat, and sprinkle in about 1 teaspoon of salt. When the salt is hot, add half the lamb, and brown the pieces well on all sides. (The salt will draw out the fat from the meat.)

3. Transfer the lamb to a 3½-quart casserole with a slotted spoon, draining the chunks of any excess fat. Brown the remaining lamb, and transfer the pieces to the casserole. Fry the onions, black beans, and garlic in the lamb fat, until browned. Transfer them to the casserole.

4. Mix the braising liquid ingredients well, and pour the liquid over the lamb and onions. Drain the bean curd sticks, cut them into 2-inch lengths, and add them to the casserole. Stir everything together until well mixed. Bring the liquid to a boil, reduce the heat to medium low, cover the casserole, and simmer the stew for 1½ hours or until lamb is done, turning the ingredients over once or twice. Discard the ginger slice.

5. Mix the cornstarch and water binder, and stir it into the liquid. Cook the sauce for a few minutes to thicken it.

6. Add the sesame oil, and give all the ingredients a final stir. Sprinkle the coriander leaves or scallion rounds over the top, and serve the stew hot.

Preparation time: 2 hours
Cooking time: 1½ hours
Serves: 4

RED-COOKED LEG OF LAMB

There is a very famous short story by Roald Dahl in which a frozen leg of lamb is the murder weapon. The murderer served the weapon to the inspectors who, by eating it, destroyed the evidence. The following recipe is not designed to incite murder — just good cooking.

Ingredients

5½ to 6-pound leg of lamb, shank and sirloin removed
2   cloves garlic, peeled and cut into slivers
    Vegetable oil for browning lamb

Braising Liquid

1   cup black soy sauce
1   cup sherry
½   teaspoon sugar
2   dried chili peppers, broken in half (use both seeds and pods)
2   whole star anise

Binder and Final Seasoning

1   teaspoon cornstarch
1   teaspoon cold water
¼   teaspoon sesame oil

Instructions

1. Make small slashes all over the leg of lamb, and insert the garlic slivers into them.

2. Put a large frying pan or a wok over high heat, and add enough oil to coat the inside (about 1½ tablespoons), tilting the pan to cover the entire cooking surface. When the oil is hot, add the lamb, and brown it on all sides (about 15 minutes).

3. Mix the braising liquid ingredients in an oval casserole large enough (4 quarts) to hold the lamb. Add the lamb to the casserole, then pour in enough water to cover the meat. Bring liquid to a boil, reduce the heat to medium low, cover the casserole, and simmer the lamb for 2 hours, or until it is cooked to the desired doneness, turning it occasionally.

4. Transfer the lamb to a serving platter, and strain 1 cup of the braising liquid into a saucepan. (The rest of the liquid can be frozen and used for other red-cooked Chinese lamb dishes.)

5. Skim any fat from the cup of liquid, and bring the liquid to a simmer. Stir the cornstarch and water binder, and mix it into the liquid. Cook the sauce, stirring, until it is thickened.

6. Stir in the sesame oil, pour the sauce over the lamb, and serve the leg of lamb hot.

Preparation time: 15 minutes
Cooking time: 2 hours
Serves: 8 to 10

LAMB CHOPS IN SOY AND MUSTARD SAUCE

Grilling is such a boring way of cooking lamb chops. Here is a recipe for a different way to prepare them. The combination of soy sauce and mustard is particularly good with this meat.

Ingredients

Vegetable oil for browning chops
4   loin lamb chops, about 1 inch thick

Braising Liquid

¼   cup black soy sauce
¼   cup sherry
¼   teaspoon sugar
2   cloves garlic, peeled and flattened
1   slice fresh ginger root, ⅛-inch thick, flattened

Binder and Final Seasoning

2   tablespoons Dijon-style mustard
1   teaspoon cornstarch
1   teaspoon cold water
¼   teaspoon sesame oil

Instructions

1. Put a large frying pan or a wok over high heat, and add enough oil to film it (about 1½ tablespoons); tilt the pan to make sure that the entire cooking surface is coated. When the oil is hot, brown the lamb chops for about 5 to 6 minutes on each side.

2. Mix the braising liquid ingredients in a casserole large enough (3 quarts) to hold the chops in 1 layer. Transfer the chops to the casserole.

3. Bring the liquid to a boil, reduce the heat to medium low, and simmer the chops for 1 hour or until done, turning them once or twice.

4. Using a slotted spoon, transfer the lamb chops to a serving platter, draining them well. Pour the liquid into a bowl or cup, discard the slice of ginger, and skim off the fat. Put the mustard into another bowl, and whisk it a few strokes. Then pour the liquid gradually into the mustard, whisking it to blend well. Pour this mixture back into the casserole, and bring it to a simmer. Stir together the cornstarch and water binder, and mix it into the liquid. Cook the sauce for a few minutes to thicken it.

5. Stir in the sesame oil, pour the sauce over the lamb chops, and serve them hot.

Preparation time: 10 minutes
Cooking time: 1¼ hours
Serves: 4

SEAFOOD

China's vast coastline and enormous networks of rivers, lakes, and ponds have made fish, mollusks, and crustaceans a very important part of the Chinese diet. It is quite possible that the Chinese were the first to farm fish; for many centuries, they have raised carp in ponds, where the fish feed on algae, weedy grasses, and other vegetation.

The Chinese also dry a great variety of seafood, including oysters, scallops, shrimp, sea cucumbers, squid, sharks' fins, sea urchins, fish maw, and fish, so that inlanders, as well as coastal dwellers, can enjoy the rich harvest of the waters. In addition, oysters are cooked down and made into oyster sauce, a major condiment in Chinese cooking. Fish and shrimp are brined and made into fermented pastes that are also used as seasonings.

Some recipes in this chapter illustrate Chinese ways of using dried seafood. And, of course, there are also recipes for fresh fish and shellfish.

POACHED FISH BALLS WITH BEAN CURD CUBES

This dish is light in texture, low in calories, and very high in protein. It is also economical.

Ingredients

1   pound fillet of flounder, diced
1   tablespoon minced ham
1   tablespoon fresh coriander leaves (no stems)
2   egg whites
2   teaspoons thin soy sauce
2   teaspoons sherry
¼   teaspoon sugar
¼   teaspoon white pepper
⅛   teaspoon finely grated fresh ginger root
½   teaspoon sesame oil
    Lettuce leaves to line casserole
2   squares bean curd, cut into 1-inch cubes

Braising Liquid

2   tablespoons thin soy sauce
2   tablespoons sherry
1   tablespoon oyster sauce
¼   cup water

Binder and Final Seasoning

2   teaspoons cornstarch
2   teaspoons cold water
¼   teaspoon sesame oil

Instructions

1. In a food processor fitted with the steel knife, assemble the flounder, ham, coriander, egg whites, soy sauce, sherry, sugar, pepper, ginger, and sesame oil, and whirl the ingredients for 60 seconds, or until the fish is minced and everything is well blended. (If you do not have a food processor, mince the fish, ham, and coriander with a Chinese cleaver or a chef's knife; then stir in the seasonings until everything is well blended.)

2. Chill the mixture in the refrigerator for 2 hours. (Chilling makes it easier for you to shape the fish balls.)

3. Line a heavy 10½-inch casserole with the lettuce leaves (see page 25).

4. Shape fish balls with your hands; make them approximately 1¼ inches in diameter. (You will have 20 to 22 fish balls.)

5. Place the fish balls and bean curd cubes in the lettuce-lined casserole. Combine the braising liquid ingredients, pour the mixture over the fish balls, and bring it to a boil over high heat. Reduce the heat to medium low, cover the pan, and simmer the casserole for 15 to 20 minutes. Do not overcook.

6. Using a slotted spoon, remove the fish balls and bean curd to a warm serving dish. Discard the lettuce leaves. Stir the cornstarch and water together, and mix the binder into the liquid. Simmer the sauce for a few minutes until it is thickened.

7. Stir in the sesame oil. Pour the sauce over the fish and bean curd, and serve the dish hot.

Preparation time: About 2¼ hours
Cooking time: 20 minutes
Serves: 4

CLAMS WITH BLACK BEAN AND GARLIC SAUCE

In Frank Chin's play <u>The Year of the Dragon</u>, which I acted in at the American Place Theatre in New York, the protagonist has a short monologue about clams. He is explaining to his sister that the only communication between him and their father is through food. I just know that the clams he is talking about are made with black bean and garlic sauce.

Ingredients

1   dozen cherrystone clams (in the shell), well scrubbed under running water

Vegetable oil for frying black bean and garlic mixture

1 ½ tablespoons salted black beans, rinsed, drained, and mashed

1   tablespoon minced garlic

Braising Liquid

1   teaspoon thin soy sauce

⅛   teaspoon finely grated fresh ginger root

¼   cup water

Binder and Final Seasoning

2   teaspoons cornstarch

2   teaspoons cold water

½   teaspoon sesame oil

Garnish

2   scallions, cut into ¼-inch rounds (use both white and green parts)

Instructions

1. Put the clams into a 4-quart casserole.

2. Combine the braising liquid ingredients.

3. Put a wok or a frying pan over high heat, and add enough oil to coat the bottom of the pan (about 1 ½ tablespoons), tilting the pan to make sure the entire cooking surface is covered. (You may need more oil, depending upon the size of the pan.) When the oil is hot, add the black beans and garlic, and fry them for about 3 minutes, stirring to keep them from sticking. Then reduce the heat to medium low, and add the mixed braising sauce ingredients.

4. Pour the sauce over the clams, and bring it to a boil over high heat. Reduce the heat to medium low, cover the casserole, and simmer the clams for 15 to 20 minutes, or until they have opened. (After the first 7 or 8 minutes, stir the clams, making sure the bottom clams go to the top and the top clams go to the bottom.)

5. When all the clams have opened, transfer them to a large serving bowl. (A pair of tongs is helpful for this.) Bring the braising liquid to a boil. Stir the cornstarch and water together, mix the binder into the sauce, and cook it for a few minutes until it thickens slightly.

6. Stir in the sesame oil. Pour the sauce over the clams, sprinkle the scallion rounds on top, and serve the clams hot.

Preparation time: About 10 minutes
Cooking time: About 20 minutes
Serves: 2 as a main course, 4 to 6 as part of a Chinese meal

RED-COOKED FISH FILLETS

If frozen fillets are the only kind of fish available to you, try this recipe for a braised dish. Of course, you can also use fresh fish.

Ingredients

Lettuce leaves to line casserole
1   pound frozen fish fillets, defrosted and patted dry

Braising Liquid

2   tablespoons thin soy sauce
2   tablespoons sherry
¼   teaspoon sugar
1   clove garlic, peeled and flattened
1   slice fresh ginger root, ⅛-inch thick, flattened
2   tablespoons oyster sauce
½   cup water

Binder and Final Seasoning

1   teaspoon cornstarch
1   teaspoon cold water
¼   teaspoon sesame oil

Instructions

1. Line a 10½-inch casserole with lettuce leaves (see page 25), and arrange the fish on them.

2. Mix the braising liquid ingredients, and pour the liquid over the fish. If it doesn't cover the fillets (this will depend upon the size and type of the fillets), mix more braising liquid, in the same proportions, to cover the fish.

3. Bring the liquid barely to a boil over high heat. Reduce the heat to medium low, cover the casserole, and simmer the fish fillets for 20 minutes. Then discard the slice of ginger.

4. Mix the cornstarch and water, and stir enough of the binder into the liquid to thicken it slightly. (Be careful not to break up the fish during this operation.)

5. Drizzle the sesame oil over the fish, and serve it hot.

Preparation time: Time to defrost fish
Cooking time: About 20 minutes
Serves: 2 to 4

DRIED OYSTERS STEWED WITH BEAN CURD STICKS

If you were snowbound in a cabin in the woods and had no fresh food but did have the dried, canned, and frozen ingredients called for in this recipe, you would not starve.

Ingredients

15 dried oysters
3 bean curd sticks (6 lengths)
8 dried black Oriental mushrooms

Braising Liquid

3 tablespoons thin soy sauce
3 tablespoons sherry
½ teaspoon sugar
1 slice fresh ginger root, ⅛-inch thick, flattened
1 cup reserved mushroom-soaking liquid (see step 1)
½ cup chicken broth (or clam broth)

Vegetables

8 water chestnuts, cut into ¼-inch dice
½ cup bamboo shoots, cut into ¼-inch dice
1 cup frozen peas

Binder

2 teaspoons cornstarch
2 teaspoons cold water

Final Seasoning

½ teaspoon sesame oil
2 tablespoons oyster sauce

Instructions

1. Cover the oysters with water, and soak them for 24 hours, changing the water twice. Before assembling the dish, drain the oysters, and cut them into ¼-inch dice. Put bean curd sticks to soak in water to cover for 2 hours. Drain them, and cut them into ½-inch lengths. Cover the mushrooms with tepid water, and soak them for 1 hour. Drain the mushrooms, reserving the liquid, cut off and discard the stems, and dice the caps into ¼-inch pieces.

2. Mix the braising liquid ingredients in a 1 ½- or 2-quart casserole. Add the diced oysters, bean curd sticks, and mushrooms. Bring the liquid to a boil over high heat. Reduce the heat to medium low, cover the casserole, and simmer the stew for 1 hour.

3. Add the water chestnuts, bamboo shoots, and peas, and mix everything well. Cover the casserole, and simmer the ingredients for another 15 minutes. Then discard the ginger slice.

4. Stir the cornstarch and water binder together, and mix it into the stew.

5. Add the sesame oil and oyster sauce, combining them well with the sauce. Simmer the stew for a few minutes to allow the sauce to thicken slightly. Serve the oyster stew hot.

Preparation time: 24 hours to soak the oysters; 2 hours to soak the other ingredients

Cooking time: 1¼ hours

Serves: 4 as a main course, 8 as part of a Chinese meal

FISH DUMPLINGS IN EGG POUCHES

This recipe is similar to Pork-filled Egg-Pouch Dumplings (see page 170), but instead of a minced pork filling, these dumplings are filled with a minced fish mixture. This is a good way to stretch a small amount of filleted fish.

Filling

½ pound flounder fillets
1 shallot (about ¾ inch in diameter)
1 egg white
2 teaspoons thin soy sauce
2 teaspoons sherry
¼ teaspoon sugar
⅛ teaspoon finely grated fresh ginger root
1 tablespoon finely minced ham (optional)
⅛ teaspoon white pepper
¼ teaspoon sesame oil

Dumpling Skins

Vegetable oil
9 large eggs, plus 1 yolk (from the egg that supplied the white for the filling), beaten

Lettuce

Lettuce leaves to line casserole

Braising Liquid

1 tablespoon thin soy sauce
1 tablespoon sherry
1 tablespoon oyster sauce
½ teaspoon sugar
½ cup fish broth (or clam broth or water)

Binder and Final Seasoning

1   teaspoon cornstarch
1   teaspoon cold water
¼   teaspoon sesame oil

Instructions

1. Combine the ingredients for the filling in a blender or food processor, and process them until the fish is minced but not puréed. If you have neither machine, mince the fish, shallot, and ham (if you include the ham) to a fine texture with a Chinese cleaver or chef's knife; then stir in the seasonings.

2. Heat a crêpe pan (or a small, heavy cast-iron skillet) until it is hot. Add enough oil just to coat the bottom of the pan. When the oil is hot, pour about 1 tablespoon of well-beaten egg into the center of the pan, and swirl the egg around until a thin omelet 2¼ to 3 inches in diameter forms in the center of the pan (see page 34).

3. When the omelet has barely started to set, place 1 scant teaspoonful of the filling in its center. Using a spatula, immediately fold the pancake over into a crescent. Press the edge of the crescent shut with the edge of the spatula. (The runny egg, pressure, and heat should seal this little dumpling shut.) Remove the filled dumpling to an oiled plate. Continue making and filling the dumpling skins until all the fish mixture is used. At this point, the dumplings can be cooled, then covered with plastic wrap and refrigerated until the next day.

4. Line a 2-quart casserole with lettuce leaves (see page 25). Layer the egg pouches in the casserole.

5. Combine the braising liquid ingredients in a saucepan, and heat the liquid until well blended and hot. When the liquid bubbles, stir the cornstarch and water binder together, and add it to the liquid.

6. Add the sesame oil, and stir to blend it well. Pour the sauce

over the dumplings, cover the casserole, and cook the contents over low heat for 15 to 20 minutes, swirling the sauce over the top layer of dumplings from time to time. Serve the dumplings hot.

Preparation time: About 1 hour
Cooking time: About 20 minutes
Yield: About 30
Serves: 4 as a main course, 8 as an appetizer

DUCK, SQUAB, CORNISH HENS, AND TURKEY

Duck is another important barnyard animal in China, so it follows that duck is important in Chinese cooking. Duck definitely enters the banquet arena for both Chinese and Westerners; to many non-Chinese, Peking Duck is the most mysterious and esoteric dish of all. Perhaps that is only logical. After all, the essence of the dish is the crisp skin; the rest of the bird is of minor significance — an almost decadent state of affairs. I once asked a non-Chinese friend what he thought of Peking duck. His reply was, "If only I knew a woman with skin like that!"

The Western cook almost always associates duck with oven cooking. The duck recipes in this chapter follow the family-style tradition of braising or simmering the duck on top of the stove, which grew out of the fact that in China there were no ovens in home kitchens.

Recipes for other things with wings such as squab, Cornish hens, and turkey are included to give variations in taste and texture.

LICHEE DUCK

Legend has it that during the Tang dynasty, the Emperor Ming spared no effort to indulge the passion of his beautiful concubine-consort Yang Kuei Fe for fresh lichee fruit, a delicacy that is in season for only about two weeks a year. He is said to have established a pony express along a 700-mile route to relay baskets of the fruit to the palace within two or three days. It is a long-winded story, but eventually Yang Kuei Fe was executed.

Ingredients

4- to 5-pound duckling (if frozen, thawed out)
Coarse (kosher) salt for browning duck
Half the fruit from 1-pound can of lichees (reserve syrup)

Braising Liquid

¼ cup black soy sauce
¼ cup sherry
1 cup reserved lichee syrup
1 whole star anise
1 dried chili pepper, broken in half (use both seeds and pod)
2 cloves garlic, peeled and flattened
1 slice fresh ginger root, ⅛-inch thick, flattened

Binder and Final Seasoning

1 tablespoon cornstarch
1 tablespoon cold water
½ teaspoon sesame oil

Instructions

1. Remove the fat from the duck's cavity. Cut off the wing tips, and save them, with the neck and gizzard, to make a duck broth if you wish; freeze the duck liver to add to your hoard for making a duck liver pâté. Rinse the duck under cold running water, drain it, and pat it dry inside and out with paper towels.

2. Put a large cast-iron skillet or a wok over high heat. Sprinkle 1 teaspoon of salt into the pan. When the salt is hot, put in the duck, breast side down. Reduce the heat to medium high. The duck will start to brown in its own fat (see page 30). Brown the duck evenly on all sides (about 10 minutes).

3. Mix the braising liquid ingredients in a 4-quart casserole. Place the duck, breast side down, in the casserole after draining it of all excess fat. (To drain and transfer the duck, insert a slotted spoon into the cavity.) Bring the liquid to a boil, then reduce the heat to medium low, cover the casserole, and simmer the duck for 1 ½ to 2 hours, turning it over from time to time.

4. When the duck is done, transfer it to a platter. Do not overcook the bird. (To tell if the duck is done, pierce the thigh with the point of a knife. If the juices are slightly pink, the duck is medium rare; if the juices are clear, it is well done.) Garnish the duck with the lichee fruit.

5. Strain the braising liquid into a small pot, and skim off the fat. Cook the liquid over moderately high heat until it is reduced by half. Mix the cornstarch and water binder, and stir it into the liquid. Cook the sauce for a few minutes, stirring it, until it is slightly thickened.

6. Stir in the sesame oil. Serve the sauce separately, or pour it over the duck. Serve the duck hot.

Preparation time: 15 minutes
Cooking time: 2 hours
Serves: 2

CURRIED BRAISED DUCK

Many people are surprised that curry is used in Chinese cooking; yet, one of my early childhood memories is of the fragrance of a slow-simmering chicken curry wafting through the house. Cantonese are very fond of curry and use it quite often in their home-style cooking.

Ingredients

Coarse (kosher) salt for browning duck
5-pound duckling, thawed if frozen, as much fat removed as possible and cut into 1½- by-2½-inch pieces
Lettuce leaves to line casserole
1 large onion, cut in half from top to bottom, peeled, and cut into ¼-inch slices along the grain

Braising Liquid

3 tablespoons thin soy sauce
3 tablespoons sherry
1 tablespoon sugar
2 tablespoons tomato catsup
2 tablespoons curry powder (or to taste)
½ teaspoon chili powder
½ cup water

Binder and Final Seasoning

1 teaspoon cornstarch
1 teaspoon cold water
½ teaspoon sesame oil

Instructions

1. Heat a large cast-iron frying pan or a wok over high heat. Sprinkle 1 to 2 teaspoons of salt into the hot pan. When the salt is hot, add half the duck pieces to the pan. Turn the pieces until they are a golden brown (7 to 10 minutes); they will brown in their own fat.

2. Line a 3- or 4-quart casserole with lettuce leaves (see page 25), and sprinkle the onion pieces over them. Put the first batch of browned duck into the casserole. Discard all the rendered duck fat in the browning pan, add 1 to 2 teaspoons fresh salt to the pan, and repeat the browning process with the remaining duck.

3. Mix the braising liquid ingredients together, stirring until the sugar is dissolved, and pour the liquid over the duck. Bring liquid to a boil, reduce the heat to medium low, cover the casserole, and simmer the duck for 1 ½ hours, turning the duck pieces from time to time.

4. When the duck is done, stir together the cornstarch and water binder, and blend it with the liquid in the casserole. (To tell if the duck is done, pierce the thigh with the point of a knife. If the juices are slightly pink, the duck is medium rare; if the juices are clear, it is well done.)

5. Stir in the sesame oil and mix well. Serve the duck hot.

Preparation time: 20 minutes
Cooking time: 1 ½ hours
Serves: 2 as a main course, 4 to 6 as part of a Chinese meal

SOY SAUCE DUCK

Many of the recipes in this chapter are for braised duck with a fruit flavor and garnish. This recipe is for a plain red-cooked duck, which is equally delicious.

Ingredients

4- to 5-pound duckling (if frozen, thawed out)
Coarse (kosher) salt for browning duck

Braising Liquid

½ cup black soy sauce
½ cup sherry
1 tablespoon sugar
2 whole star anise
1 dried chili pepper, broken in half (use both seeds and pod)
2 cloves garlic, peeled and flattened
1 slice fresh ginger root, ⅛-inch thick, flattened

Binder and Final Seasoning

1 ½ teaspoons cornstarch
1 ½ teaspoons cold water
½ teaspoon sesame oil

Instructions

1. Remove the fat from the duck's cavity. Cut off the wing tips, and save them, with the neck and gizzard, to make a duck broth if you wish; freeze the duck liver to add to your hoard for making a duck liver pâté. Rinse the duck under cold running water, drain it, and pat it dry inside and out with paper towels.

2. Put a large, heavy frying pan or a wok over high heat, and sprinkle about 1 teaspoon of salt into it. When the salt is hot, put the duck in, breast side down. Reduce the heat to medium high. The duck will start to brown in its own fat (see page 30). Brown the duck on all sides (about 10 minutes).

3.   While the duck is browning, mix the braising liquid ingredients in a 4-quart casserole.

4.   Place the browned duck, breast side down, in the casserole. (To drain and transfer the duck, insert a slotted spoon in the cavity.) Bring the liquid to a boil over high heat; then reduce the heat to low, cover the casserole, and simmer the duck for 1 hour. Turn the duck on its back, and simmer it for 1 more hour.

5.   Transfer the duck to a serving platter. Strain the braising liquid and return 1 cup of it to the casserole. (The remaining liquid can be frozen and used for any of the red-cooked dishes in this book.)

6.   Mix the cornstarch and water binder, and stir it into the liquid. Cook the sauce for a few minutes to allow it to thicken slightly. (If a thicker sauce is desired, add ½ teaspoon each of cornstarch and water to the liquid.)

7.   Add the sesame oil, and mix well. Serve the duck hot, with the sauce in a gravy boat.

Preparation time: 15 minutes
Cooking time: 2 hours
Serves: 2 as a main dish, 4 to 6 as part of a Chinese meal

SPICY HOISIN DUCK

Instead of being cooked whole, the duck for this dish is cut into small pieces, browned, then braised in a pungent sauce. Adjust the amount of chili peppers according to how hot you want the dish to be.

Ingredients

6   dried black Oriental mushrooms
    Coarse (kosher) salt for browning duck
    4- to 5-pound duckling (if frozen, thawed out), cut into 1½-by-3-inch pieces, with as much fat removed as possible
1   large onion, cut in half from the top to bottom, peeled, and cut into ¼-inch slices along the grain
½   cup sliced bamboo shoots

Braising Liquid

¼   cup black soy sauce
¼   cup sherry
¼   teaspoon sugar
2   cloves garlic, peeled and flattened
1   slice fresh ginger root, ⅛-inch thick, flattened
¼   teaspoon five-spice powder
5   tablespoons hoisin sauce
3   dried chili peppers, broken in half (use both seeds and pods)
½   cup mushroom-soaking liquid (see step 1)

Binder and Final Seasoning

1½ teaspoons cornstarch
1½ teaspoons cold water
½   teaspoon sesame oil

Garnish

2   scallions, cut into ¼-inch rounds (use both green and white parts)

Instructions

1. Soak the dried mushrooms in warm water to cover for 1 hour. Drain the mushrooms, reserving the soaking liquid, cut off and discard the stems, and quarter the mushroom caps.

2. Put a large cast-iron frying pan or a wok over high heat. Sprinkle 1 teaspoon of salt into the pan. When the salt is hot, add the duck pieces. Keep moving the pieces over high heat with a spatula and a slotted spoon (you really need both utensils) until the duck is browned all over (about 8 minutes). Add the onion and mushrooms to the pan while you are browning the duck.

3. Meanwhile, mix the braising liquid in a 3- to 4-quart casserole. Transfer the duck, mushrooms, and onion to the casserole, using a slotted spoon to drain them well of any fat. Bring the liquid to a boil, lower the heat to medium low, cover the casserole, and simmer the duck for 1 ½ hours.

4. Transfer the duck, onion, and mushrooms to a serving bowl with a slotted spoon. Skim the liquid of all fat, and discard the ginger slice. Add the bamboo shoots. Mix the cornstarch and water binder, and stir it into the liquid. Cook the sauce for a few minutes until it is slightly thickened.

5. Stir in the sesame oil. Pour the sauce over the duck pieces. Sprinkle the scallion rounds over the duck, and serve it hot.

Preparation time: 1 hour to soak mushrooms; 10 minutes to brown the duck
Cooking time: 2 hours
Serves: 2 as a main dish, 4 to 6 as part of a Chinese meal

WEST LAKE DUCK

The West Lake at Hangchow is famous for its beautiful scenery and floating restaurants. Hangchow itself is well known for its tradition of fine cooking, and West Lake Duck is one of its more notable specialties. A banquet dish, this duck is usually deep-fried, steamed, and served boned. This version is less complicated, but the results are equally delicious.

Ingredients

6   dried black Oriental mushrooms
     4- to 5-pound duckling (if frozen, thawed out)
     Coarse (kosher) salt for browing duck

Braising Liquid

½   cup black soy sauce
1   cup sherry
1   tablespoon honey
2   cloves garlic, peeled and flattened
1   slice fresh ginger root, ⅛-inch thick, flattened
3   whole star anise
2   or 3 pieces dried tangerine peel
1   dried chili pepper, broken in half (use both seeds and pod)
2   ribs celery, cut in half
1   medium-sized onion, whole and unpeeled
1   cup reserved mushroom-soaking liquid (see step 1)

Vegetables

½   cup sliced bamboo shoots

Binder and Final Seasonings

1   tablespoon cornstarch
1   tablespoon cold water
½   teaspoon sesame oil
2   tablespoons oyster sauce

Garnish

     Fresh coriander leaves or fresh parsley

Instructions

1. Cover the mushrooms with warm water, and soak them for 1 hour. Drain the mushrooms, and reserve the soaking liquid. Remove and discard the stems, and quarter the caps.

2. Remove the surplus fat from the duck cavity. Cut off the wing tips, and save them, along with the neck and gizzard, to make a duck broth; freeze the duck liver to make a duck liver pâté. Rinse the duck under cold running water, and pat it dry inside and out with paper towels.

3. Put a large cast-iron frying pan or a wok over a high flame, and sprinkle 1 teaspoon of salt into it. When the salt is hot, place the duck in it, breast side down, and brown the duck on all sides (about 10 minutes) (see page 30).

4. Meanwhile, mix the braising liquid ingredients in a 4-quart casserole, and bring the liquid to a boil. Reduce the heat to medium low. Insert a slotted spoon into the duck cavity, lift and drain the duck. Place the duck in the casserole, breast side down. Add enough hot water to cover the duck, mixing it well with the braising liquid. Bring the liquid to a boil, reduce the heat to medium low, cover the casserole, and simmer for 2½ to 3 hours, turning it over once or twice.

5. Transfer the duck to a serving platter. Strain 2 cups of the braising liquid into a small saucepan, and skim off the fat. Add the mushrooms and bamboo shoots, and simmer the liquid until the mushrooms are cooked (5 to 8 minutes). Mix the cornstarch and water binder, and stir it into the liquid. Cook the sauce until it is slightly thickened.

6. Add the sesame oil and oyster sauce. Pour the sauce over the duck (or serve it on the side). Garnish the duck with the coriander leaves, and serve it hot.

Preparation time: 1 hour to soak mushrooms; 10 minutes to brown the duck
Cooking time: 2½ to 3 hours
Serves: 2 as a main course, 4 to 6 as part of a Chinese meal

ORANGE DUCK

The remaining duck recipes in this chapter follow a general
format with variations. Rather than giving a master recipe and
adding "for duck with − − −, substitute − − − for − − −
(see page xyz)," I thought it would be more convenient for you if
I gave a separate recipe for each variation. I personally find it
annoying to have to flip pages back and forth. In reading this
series of recipes, you may get ideas for using other fruits. By all
means experiment with them, using these recipes as a guide.

Ingredients

4- to 5-pound duckling (if frozen, thawed out)
Coarse (kosher) salt for browning duck
1   large eating orange, peeled and cut into ¼-inch slices
     (reserve the peel, removing as much pulp as possible)

Braising Liquid

¼   cup black soy sauce
¼   cup sherry
1   cup orange juice
     Peel of 1 orange
1   whole star anise
1   dried chili pepper, broken in half (use both seeds and pod)
2   cloves garlic, peeled and flattened
1   slice fresh ginger root, ⅛-inch thick, flattened

Binder and Final Seasoning

2   teaspoons cornstarch
2   teaspoons cold water
½   teaspoon sesame oil

Instructions

1.   Remove all surplus fat from the duck cavity. Remove the
     wing tips and save them, along with the gizzard and neck,
     for duck broth; freeze the duck liver toward the day when
     you have accumulated enough to make a duck liver pâté.

Rinse the duck under cold running water, drain it, and pat it dry inside and out with paper towels.

2. Place a large cast-iron skillet or a wok over high heat. Sprinkle 1 teaspoon coarse salt into the pan. When the salt is hot, put in the duck, breast side down, and reduce the heat to medium high. The heat and the salt will draw the fat from under the skin (see page 30). It will take about 10 minutes to brown the duck, which you should turn often.

3. Meanwhile, mix the braising liquid ingredients in a 4-quart casserole.

4. When the entire surface of the duck is browned, drain off the fat, and transfer the duck, breast side down, to the casserole. (To do this, insert a slotted spoon in the cavity.) Bring the liquid to a boil, reduce the heat to medium low, cover the casserole, and simmer the duck for 1½ to 2 hours, turning the duck over from time to time.

5. When the duck is done, transfer it to a platter. (To tell if the duck is done, pierce the thigh with the point of a knife. If the juices are slightly pink, the duck is medium rare; if the juices are clear, it is well done.) Strain the liquid into a smaller pot. Skim off the fat, and reduce the liquid by half over moderately high heat.

6. Mix the cornstarch and water binder, and stir it into the liquid. Cook the sauce for a few minutes to allow it to thicken slightly.

7. Add the sesame oil, and give all the ingredients a final stir. Garnish the duck with the orange slices, and serve the sauce on the side, or pour it over the duck.

Preparation time: 15 minutes
Cooking time: About 2 hours
Serves: 2 as a main course, 4 to 6 as part of a Chinese meal

LEMON DUCK

Duck is a bird that can be used to good advantage in a variation of Lemon Chicken (see page 126).

Ingredients

4- to 5-pound duckling (if frozen, thawed out)
Coarse (kosher) salt for browning duck

Braising Liquid

¼ cup black soy sauce
½ cup sherry
1 cup water
¼ teaspoon sugar
2 cloves garlic, peeled and flattened
1 slice fresh ginger root, ⅛-inch thick, flattened
½ teaspoon five-spice powder
1 chili pepper, broken in half (use both seeds and pod)

Lemon Sauce

¾ cup lemon juice
¾ cup sugar
Grated rind of 1 lemon
1 tablespoon cornstarch
1 tablespoon cold water

Garnish

1 scallion, cut into ¼-inch rounds (use both white and green parts)

Instructions

1. Remove the fat from the duck's cavity. Cut off the wing tips, and save them, along with the neck and gizzard, to make a duck broth; freeze the duck liver, and store it until you have accumulated enough to make a duck liver pâté. Rinse the duck under cold running water, drain it, and pat it dry inside and out with paper towels.

2. Put a large, heavy frying pan or a wok over high heat, and sprinkle about 1 teaspoon of salt into it. When the salt is hot, place the duck in the pan, breast side down, and reduce the heat to medium high. Brown the duck on all sides in its own fat (see page 30) (about 10 minutes).

3. Meanwhile, mix the braising liquid in a 4-quart casserole.

4. Insert a slotted spoon in the duck's cavity, lift and drain the duck, and place it in the casserole, breast side down. Bring the braising liquid to a boil over high heat. Reduce the heat to medium low, cover the casserole, and simmer the duck for 1 hour. Turn the duck onto its back, and simmer it for 1 hour longer.

5. While the duck is simmering, put the lemon juice, sugar, and grated lemon rind in a small saucepan, and cook the mixture over moderate heat until the sugar is dissolved. Continue to cook the sauce over low heat for 15 minutes. Stir the cornstarch and water together, and mix it into the lemon sauce. Cook the sauce for a few more minutes, stirring until it has thickened slightly.

6. Transfer the duck to a serving platter, and serve the warm lemon sauce on the side. Or you can cut the duck into small pieces, reassemble it on a platter, and pour the lemon sauce over it. (The braising liquid can be frozen and reused.) Garnish the duck with the scallion rounds.

Preparation time: 10 minutes
Cooking time: 2 hours
Serves: 3 as a main course, 6 as part of a Chinese meal

DUCK WITH PEACHES

Some food authorities feel that the peach Is probably of Chinese origin. It figures quite prominently in Chinese stories and legends as a symbol of good luck. It is known that the fruit has been cultivated in China for at least 1,500 years. The peach seems to have spread westward rapidly — and right onto your table, if you cook this dish.

Ingredients

4- to 5-pound duckling (if frozen, thawed out)
Coarse (kosher) salt for browning duck
2 medium-sized peaches, peeled, sliced, and covered with water containing juice of half a lemon (to keep peaches from turning brown) (or 1 small can peach halves)
Syrup from canned peaches (if used)

Braising Liquid

¼ cup black soy sauce
¼ cup sherry
1 cup canned peach nectar (or reserved canned peach syrup)
1 whole star anise
1 dried chili pepper, broken in half (use both seeds and pod)
2 cloves garlic, peeled and flattened
1 slice fresh ginger root, ⅛-inch thick, flattened

Binder

1 ½ teaspoons cornstarch
1 ½ teaspoons cold water

Final Seasoning

½ teaspoon sesame oil

Instructions

1. Remove excess fat from the duck cavity. Remove the wing tips, and save them, along with the neck and the gizzard, to make duck broth; freeze the duck liver until you have

accumulated enough to make a liver pâté. Rinse the duck under cold running water, drain it, and pat it dry inside and out with paper towels.

2. Put a large cast-iron skillet or a wok over high heat. Sprinkle 1 teaspoon of salt into the pan. When the salt is hot, place the duck in the pan breast side down. Reduce the heat to medium high, and turn the duck (see page 30) so that the entire surface is browned (8 to 10 minutes).

3. Mix the braising liquid ingredients in a 4-quart casserole. Insert a slotted spoon in the duck's cavity, drain the duck, and transfer it to the casserole, breast side down. Bring the liquid to a boil, reduce the heat to medium low, cover the casserole, and simmer the duck for 1 ½ to 2 hours, turning it with tongs every so often.

4. When the duck is done, transfer it to a serving platter. (To tell if the duck is done, pierce the thigh with the point of a knife. If the juices are slightly pink, the duck is medium rare; if the juices are clear, it is well done.)

5. Strain the braising liquid into a smaller pot, and skim off the fat. Put the pot over medium-high heat, and reduce the liquid by half. Combine the cornstarch and water, and add the mixture to the reduced liquid. Cook the sauce for a few minutes to thicken it slightly.

6. Add the sesame oil, and give all the ingredients a final stir. Serve the sauce on the side, or pour it over the duck. Garnish the duck with the drained peach slices, and carve it at the table.

Preparation time: 10 minutes
Cooking time: About 2 hours
Serves: 2 as a main course, 4 to 6 as part of a Chinese meal

PINEAPPLE DUCK

In the movie <u>The Hawaiians</u> Charlton Heston smuggles some pineapples from South America to Hawaii, where he gives them to Tina Chen who has a green thumb. Her thumb was so green that today Hawaii seems mostly to be associated with pineapples. I dedicate this recipe to my family in Hawaii — Earll, Joseph, and Maxine Hong Kingston.

Ingredients

Coarse (kosher) salt for browning duck
4- to 5-pound duckling (if frozen, thawed out)
8-ounce can pineapple slices (reserve syrup)

Braising Liquid

¼ cup black soy sauce
¼ cup sherry
1 cup reserved pineapple syrup
1 whole star anise
1 dried chili pepper, broken in half (use both seeds and pod)
2 cloves garlic, peeled and flattened
1 slice fresh ginger root, ⅛-inch thick, flattened

Binder and Final Seasoning

1 ½ teaspoons cornstarch
1 ½ teaspoons cold water
½ teaspoon sesame oil

Instructions

1. Remove all excess fat from the duck cavity. Cut off the wing tips, and save them, with the gizzard and neck, to make a duck broth; freeze the duck liver, with any others you have accumulated, until you have enough to make a duck liver pâté. Rinse the duck under cold running water, drain it, and pat it dry inside and out with paper towels.

2. Place a large cast-iron skillet or a wok over high heat. Sprinkle 1 teaspoon of salt into the pan. When the salt is

hot, put the duck in the pan, breast side down. Reduce the heat to medium high. The duck will start to brown in its own fat, which the salt will draw out (see page 30). Turn the duck from time to time to brown it evenly on all sides (about 10 minutes).

3. Meanwhile, mix the braising liquid ingredients in a 4-quart casserole.

4. When the duck is nicely browned, drain off the fat and transfer the bird to the casserole, breast side down. Insert a slotted spoon in the duck cavity, lift and drain the duck, and pat off any excess fat with paper towels. Bring the liquid to a boil, reduce the heat to medium low, cover the casserole, and simmer the duck for 1½ to 2 hours, turning it occasionally.

5. When the duck is done, transfer it to a serving platter, and keep it warm. (To tell if the duck is done, pierce the thigh with the point of a knife. If the juices are slightly pink, the duck is medium rare; if the juices are clear, it is well done.) Strain the braising liquid into a smaller pot, and skim off the fat. Cook the liquid over moderately high heat until the volume is reduced by half.

6. Mix the cornstarch and water, and stir the binder into the liquid. Cook the sauce for a few minutes, stirring it, until it is slightly thickened.

7. Add the sesame oil, and give all the ingredients a final swirl. Serve the sauce separately or poured over the duck. Garnish the duck with the pineapple slices.

Preparation time: 10 minutes
Cooking time: 2 hours
Serves: 2 as a main course, 4 to 6 as part of a Chinese meal

RED-COOKED DUCK WITH APPLES

Although apples are not usually associated with Chinese cooking, there seem to have been apples in China even in ancient times. In fact, a Chinese candy I remember from my childhood was made from haw apples. This candy was in the shape of thin disks the size of a quarter and packaged in a tight cylinder. So why not red-cooked duck with apples?

Ingredients

4- to 5-pound duckling (if frozen, thawed out)
Coarse (kosher) salt for browning duck
2 apples, peeled and cut into ¼ inch slices

Braising Liquid

¼ cup black soy sauce
¼ cup sherry
1 cup bottled apple juice
1 whole star anise
1 dried chili pepper, broken in half (use both seeds and pod)
2 cloves garlic, peeled and flattened
1 slice fresh ginger root, ⅛-inch thick, flattened

Binder

1½ teaspoons cornstarch
1½ teaspoons cold water

Final Seasoning

½ teaspoon sesame oil

Instructions

1. Remove the fat from the duck cavity. Cut off the wing tips, and save them, with the neck and gizzard, to make duck broth; freeze the duck liver until you accumulate enough to make a duck liver pâté. Rinse the duck under cold running water, drain it, and pat it dry with paper towels.

2. Put a large heavy cast-iron skillet or a wok over high heat. Sprinkle about 1 teaspoon of salt into the pan. When the salt is hot, put in the duck, breast side down. Reduce the heat to medium high. The salt and the heat will draw the subcutaneous fat from the duck (see page 30), so that the bird will brown in its own fat. Brown the duck on all sides (about 10 minutes).

3. Meanwhile, mix the braising liquid ingredients in a 4-quart casserole.

4. Insert a slotted spoon in the duck's cavity, lift and drain it, and transfer the duck to the casserole, breast side down. Bring the liquid to a boil, reduce the heat to medium low, cover the casserole, and simmer the duck for 1½ to 2 hours, turning it from time to time.

5. When the duck is done, transfer it to a serving platter. (To tell if the duck is done, pierce the thigh with the point of a knife. If the juices are slightly pink, the duck is medium rare; if the juices are clear, it is well done.) Strain the liquid into a small pot, and skim off the fat. Cook the liquid over medium-high heat until the volume is reduced by half.

6. Mix the cornstarch and water binder, and stir it into the liquid. Cook the sauce for a few minutes to allow it to thicken slightly.

7. Stir in the sesame oil. Serve the sauce separately or pour it over the duck. Garnish the duck with the apple slices.

Preparation time: 15 minutes
Cooking time: About 2 hours
Serves: 2 as a main course, 4 to 6 as part of a Chinese meal

RED-COOKED SQUAB

Squab is much loved by the Chinese, and it is often served at banquets. This is a recipe for one of the simpler ways of cooking the bird.

Braising Liquid

1   cup black soy sauce
½   cup sherry
2   tablespoons sugar
2   whole star anise
1   dried chili pepper, broken in half (use both seeds and pod)
2   cloves garlic, peeled and flattened
1   slice fresh ginger root, ⅛-inch thick, flattened
1½ cups water

Squabs

2   squabs, cleaned and left whole

Binder and Final Seasoning

1½ teaspoons cornstarch
1½ teaspoons cold water
¼   teaspoon sesame oil

Instructions

1. Mix the braising liquid in a 1½ to 2-quart casserole, and bring it to a boil.

2. Put the two squabs into the casserole, breasts down. Reduce the heat to medium low, cover the casserole, and simmer the squabs for 30 minutes. Turn the squabs onto their backs, and simmer them for another 10 to 15 minutes.

3. Remove the squabs to a serving platter. Skim off the fat from the braising liquid. Strain 1 cup of the liquid into a small saucepan and heat it to simmering. Remaining liquid can be frozen and used for other red-cooked recipes.

4. Stir the cornstarch and water together, and mix it into the liquid. Cook the sauce for a few minutes to allow it to thicken slightly.

5. Stir in the sesame oil. Serve the squabs hot, with the sauce on the side.

Preparation time: 5 minutes
Cooking time: About 40 minutes
Serves: 2

PIQUANT SALT-BAKED CORNISH HEN

This is a variation of Salt-cooked Chicken (see page 112). The game hens are marinated, then rubbed with a thick coating of Dijon-style mustard. The hens are put into a paper bag, buried in a casserole of hot salt, and cooked on top of the stove.

Marinade

1   tablespoon thin soy sauce
1   tablespoon sherry
¼   teaspoon sugar
1   large clove garlic, peeled and flattened
1   slice fresh ginger root, ⅛-inch thick, flattened
¼   teaspoon sesame oil

Other Ingredients

2   Cornish game hens, cleaned and kept whole
    Dijon-style mustard
    4-to-6-pounds coarse (kosher) salt
    Brown paper bag large enough to hold both hens

Garnish

    Fresh watercress (or sprigs of fresh parsley)

Instructions

1. Mix the marinade, and marinate the game hens at room temperature for at least 1 hour, turning them from time to time so that they are well coated. Dry the birds with paper towels.

2. Rub the Dijon-style mustard over the hens, making a thick coating.

3. Heat 2 to 3 pounds of salt in a 4-quart casserole, or a pot large enough to hold the hens and still cover them with salt. Heat the remaining salt in a frying pan. Use medium-high heat for about ½ hour.

4. Put the hens in a brown paper bag, and twist the open end of the bag closed. Place the bag in the hot salt in the casserole, with the hens breast side down. Pour enough hot salt from the frying pan over the paper bag to bury it completely. Cover the pot and cook the hens over medium heat for about 1 hour. (To tell if the Cornish hens are done, pierce thigh with the point of a knife. If the juices are slightly pink, the bird is medium rare; if the juices are clear, it is well done.)

5. Remove the bag from the salt, using tongs, and remove the hens from the bag. (You may find some of the skin sticking to the bag.) Cover any broken skin sections with the watercress or parsley. Serve the Cornish hens hot.

Preparation time: 1 hour
Cooking time: About 1 hour
Serves: 2

POT-ROASTED TURKEY STUFFED WITH EIGHT-JEWEL RICE

Turkey is not usually associated with Chinese cuisine because it is native to the New World, but then so are corn and tomatoes, which have certainly made their way into Chinese cooking. Chinese-Americans roast turkeys at Thanksgiving, although the stuffing is usually rice-based and includes Chinese ingredients. The turkey carcass, with whatever leftover meat there is, is saved to make <u>jook</u> (see Congee, page 274) the next day. Here is a pot-roasted version of the national bird, the moistest turkey I have ever had.

Ingredients

Eight-Jewel Rice (see page 258)
10-pound young turkey (reserve gizzard, heart, and liver for sauce)
Vegetable oil to brown turkey
Lettuce leaves to line casserole

Braising Liquid

1 cup black soy sauce
1 cup sherry
1½ teaspoons sugar
3 cloves garlic, peeled and flattened
2 whole star anise
2 dried chili peppers, broken in half (use both seeds and pods)
1 slice fresh ginger root, ⅛-inch thick, flattened
2 cups water

Binder and Final Seasoning

1 tablespoon cornstarch
1 tablespoon cold water
½ teaspoon sesame oil

Instructions

1. Prepare the Eight-Jewel Rice, and set it aside. (You can prepare the rice the day before and refrigerate it. If you do this, let the rice warm to room temperature before you stuff the turkey.)

2. Pack the rice stuffing loosely into the body cavity and neck cavity; sew up the openings.

3. Pat the turkey dry. Heat enough oil (about 1 ½ tablespoons) to coat a skillet or a wok large enough to hold the turkey, tilting the pan to film the cooking surface. When the oil is hot, reduce the heat to medium high, and brown as much of the surface of the turkey as possible.

4. Line an 8-quart Dutch oven or covered pot with lettuce leaves (see page 25), and place the turkey in the pot, breast side down.

5. Mix the braising liquid ingredients and pour the liquid over the turkey.

6. Bring the liquid to a boil over high heat. Reduce the heat to medium low, cover the pot, and simmer the turkey for 3 hours, turning it after every half hour's cooking, first onto one side, then onto the other, then onto its back for the final hour.

7. During the last hour of simmering, add the gizzard, liver, and heart to the liquid. After 1 hour, remove the giblets and chop them fine.

8. To see if the turkey is done, cut into the thickest part of the thigh; if meat does not look red and the juices run clear, the

turkey is done. Do <u>not</u> overcook. Remove the turkey to a warm platter. Remove the threads, and carefully transfer the stuffing to a serving bowl.

9.   Remove the lettuce leaves from the braising liquid with a slotted spoon, and discard them. Strain the liquid, and put it into a small saucepan. Add the chopped liver, heart, and gizzard to the liquid. Simmer the liquid for a few minutes. Mix the cornstarch and water binder, stir it into the liquid, and cook until lightly thickened.

10. If the sauce is not thick enough, mix and add more cornstarch and water. Stir in the sesame oil.

11. The turkey is not going to look like a photograph put out by the American Turkey Institute, if there is such a body, so I advise you to carve it in the kitchen, arrange the slices attractively on a large platter, and spoon the sauce over the slices. Or serve the sauce separately in a gravy boat. Serve the turkey hot, with the Eight-Jewel Rice stuffing.

Preparation time: About 1 hour
Cooking time: 3 hours
Serves: 10

COMBINATION POTS

The dishes in this chapter are economical to prepare. They make use of leftovers and stretch small amounts of meat, seafood, and vegetables that blend to provide harmonious contrasts in taste, texture, and color, qualities that are very important to the Chinese. These combination pots are mostly soupy or moist in consistency, and most need no binder. The variety of combinations should give you an idea of how you can improvise and invent your own combination pots. All the recipes in this section will serve two generously. If you wish to serve more people, either double the quantity or serve several combination pots for dinner.

FIVE-JEWEL CASSEROLE

The Chinese often make harmonious combinations of unlikely ingredients and give them poetic descriptive names, such as Eight Jade or Triple Dragon. A lot is left to the inventiveness of the chef. The Chinese consider three, five, and eight to be lucky numbers, so I call this dish Five-Jewel Casserole.

Ingredients

15 dried oysters

Braising Liquid

2 tablespoons thin soy sauce
2 tablespoons sherry
½ teaspoon sugar
1 tablespoon oyster sauce
½ cup reserved oyster-soaking liquid (see step 2)

Remaining Four Jewels

6 deep-fried bean curd squares, cut in half
3 to 4 ounces Chinese barbecued pork, cut into ⅛-inch slices (see page 168)
6 water chestnuts, sliced
¼ pound fresh snow peas (if small, leave whole; if large, cut in half on the diagonal)

Binder and Final Seasoning

1 teaspoon cornstarch
1 teaspoon cold water
¼ teaspoon sesame oil

Instructions

1. Cover the oysters with water, and soak them for 24 hours, changing the water twice.

2. Drain the oysters (reserve the liquid), and put them into a 1½-quart casserole. Combine the braising liquid ingredients, and pour the mixture over the oysters. Bring the liquid to a boil over high heat, lower heat, cover the casserole, and simmer the oysters for 30 minutes.

3. Add the fried bean curd squares, and mix them well with the oysters. Cover the pot, and simmer the ingredients for 15 minutes.

4. Add the barbecued pork, water chestnuts, and snow peas, and simmer the casserole 5 minutes.

5. Stir the cornstarch and water binder together, and mix it into the casserole.

6. Stir in the sesame oil, and cook the stew for a few minutes until the sauce thickens slightly. Serve the casserole hot.

Preparation time: 24 hours to soak the oysters, 5 minutes to assemble the dish
Cooking time: 50 minutes
Serves: 2 as a main course, 4 to 6 as part of a Chinese meal

HIGH-PROTEIN CASSEROLE

This casserole is high in protein, low in cost, and takes the austerity out of a high-protein diet. Omit the star anise if you don't like its licorice taste.

Ingredients

Lettuce leaves to line casserole
2 pork chops (about ½ pound) cut into ½-inch cubes
3 hard-cooked eggs, peeled
1 square fresh bean curd, cut into ½-inch cubes
¼ cup bamboo shoots, cut into ½-inch cubes
1 small onion, cut in half from top to bottom, peeled, and cut into ¼-inch slices along the grain

Braising Liquid

2 tablespoons black soy sauce
2 tablespoons sherry
½ teaspoon sugar
2 cloves garlic, finely minced
⅛ teaspoon freshly grated ginger root
1 whole star anise
¼ cup chicken broth

Final Seasoning

¼ teaspoon sesame oil

Instructions

1. Line a 1-quart casserole with lettuce leaves (see page 25).

2. Put the cubed pork, hard-cooked eggs, bean curd, bamboo shoots, and onion into the casserole.

3. Mix the braising liquid ingredients well, and pour the liquid over the ingredients in the casserole. Bring the liquid to a boil over medium high heat. Reduce the heat to medium low, cover the casserole, and simmer the contents for ½ hour.

4. Stir the ingredients, and simmer them for another ½ hour.

5. Drizzle the sesame oil over the contents of the casserole, give everything a final stir, and serve the casserole hot.

Preparation time: 25 minutes, including 15 minutes to cook the eggs
Cooking time: 1 hour
Serves: 2

NO NAME CASSEROLE

You may have noticed that a number of recipes have in their titles the number three, five, or eight. Chinese are superstitious, and consider these lucky numbers. But the number four has the same sound in Chinese as the word for "dead." That is why there are no "Four-Jewel" or "Four Precious" casseroles in this book, and why there is no name for this casserole.

Ingredients

Lettuce to line casserole
½ pound chicken livers, blanched in boiling water for 3 minutes
½ pound shrimp, peeled and deveined
¼ pound barbecued pork, cut into ¼-inch slices (see page 168)
½ can straw mushrooms, drained

Braising Liquid

2 tablespoons thin soy sauce
2 tablespoons sherry
½ teaspoon sugar
2 cloves garlic, finely minced
⅛ teaspoon freshly grated ginger root
⅛ teaspoon white pepper
2 tablespoons oyster sauce
¼ cup chicken broth

Final Seasoning

¼ teaspoon sesame oil

Instructions

1. Line a 1-quart casserole with lettuce leaves (see page 25).

2. Add the blanched chicken livers, shrimp, barbecued pork, and straw mushrooms to the casserole.

3. Mix the braising liquid ingredients well, and pour the liquid over the ingredients in the casserole. Bring the liquid to a boil over medium-high heat. Reduce the heat to medium low, cover the casserole, and simmer the contents for ½ hour.

4. Stir in the sesame oil, give all the ingredients a final stir, and serve the casserole hot.

Preparation time: 10 minutes
Cooking time: 30 minutes
Serves: 2

Note: For a colorful variation, add ¼ pound snow peas during the last 5 minutes of cooking.

EIGHT-JADE CASSEROLE

One of the outstanding characteristics of Chinese cooking is the combination of various meats, seafood, and other ingredients to make a dish that is harmonious in texture, taste, and visual appeal. "Eight Jade" is a popular description with chefs because eight is considered a lucky number and jade is a precious stone. Feel free to make substitutions of your choice.

Ingredients

4   dried black Oriental mushrooms
    Lettuce leaves for lining casserole
8   shrimp, peeled and deveined
4   chicken livers, trimmed and cut in half
8   chicken hearts
4   chicken gizzards, cut in half
4   small squid, cleaned and cut into 1-inch pieces
    Vegetable oil
8   slices Chinese barbecued pork (about ¼ pound) (see page 168)
1   cup frozen peas, thawed

Marinade

2   tablespoons thin soy sauce
2   tablespoons sherry
¼   teaspoon sugar
2   cloves garlic, peeled and finely minced
⅛   teaspoon grated fresh ginger root
¼   teaspoon sesame oil

Braising Liquid

½   cup mushroom-soaking liquid (see step 1)
½   cup chicken broth
3   tablespoons oyster sauce
¼   teaspoon white pepper

Binder

2   teaspoons cornstarch
2   teaspoons cold water

Final Seasoning

¼   teaspoon sesame oil

Instructions

1. Cover the dried mushrooms with warm water and soak them for 1 hour. Drain the mushrooms, reserving the soaking liquid. Then remove and discard the stems, and quarter the mushroom caps.

2. Line a 2½-quart casserole with lettuce leaves (see page 25).

3. Mix the marinade ingredients together, stirring them until the sugar dissolves. Put the shrimp, chicken livers, hearts, gizzards, and squid in one bowl, cover them with the marinade, and marinate for 1 hour at room temperature.

4. Put a frying pan or a wok over high heat, and add enough vegetable oil (about 1 tablespoon), to cover the cooking surface. When the oil is hot, put the marinated ingredients in the pan, and stir-fry them over medium-high heat until the livers and gizzards are a brownish color.

5. Transfer the stir-fried ingredients to the casserole, and add the mushrooms, barbecued pork, and peas.

6. Combine the braising liquid ingredients, and pour the mixture into the casserole. Bring the liquid to a boil over high heat. Reduce the heat to medium low, cover the casserole, and simmer the ingredients for ½ hour.

7. Stir the cornstarch and water together to make a binder, and mix it into the liquid. Stir in the sesame oil, and cook the sauce for a few minutes to thicken slightly. Serve hot.

Preparation time: About 1 hour
Cooking time: 30 minutes
Serves: 3

BUDDHA'S DELIGHT VEGETARIAN CASSEROLE

Each restaurant has its own version of this vegetarian dish, which makes use of dried, canned, and some fresh vegetable products. Some restaurants use as many as seventeen ingredients. In this version, the major seasoning is the white bean curd cheese. This could also be a clean-out-the-refrigerator dish.

Ingredients

4   dried black Oriental mushrooms
    2-ounce package cellophane noodles
8   cloud ears
6   golden needles
6   dried bean curd skins
    Lettuce leaves to line casserole
¼   cup sliced bamboo shoots
¼   cup sliced water chestnuts
    10-ounce can braised gluten (mock abalone) or "vegetarian steak"
3   ounces snow peas, trimmed and cut in half (or ½ cup broccoli flowerets)

Braising Liquid

2   tablespoons thin soy sauce
4   tablespoons sherry
1   teaspoon sugar
2   squares white bean curd cheese (more if you like a stronger flavor)
½   cup mushroom-soaking liquid (see step 1)
½   cup water

Final Seasoning

½   teaspoon sesame oil

Instructions

1. Cover the mushrooms with warm water, and soak them for 1 hour. Drain the mushrooms, reserving the soaking liquid, remove and discard the stems, and cut the caps into quarters. Soak the cellophane noodles in warm water for ½ hour; drain them well. Soak the cloud ears in warm water for ½ hour; drain them well. Cover the golden needles with warm water, and soak them for ½ hour; drain them well. Soak the bean curd skins in warm water for ½ hour. Drain them well, and cut them into quarters.

2. Line a 1½-quart casserole with the lettuce leaves (see page 25). Put all the ingredients except the snow peas or broccoli on top of the lettuce.

3. Mix the braising liquid ingredients well, mashing the white bean curd cheese, and pour the liquid over the ingredients. Stir to blend everything well. Bring the liquid to a boil over high heat. Reduce the heat to medium low, cover the casserole, simmer the contents for ½ hour. Add the broccoli if you are using it and simmer the ingredients for another 10 minutes (longer if you don't like your broccoli crunchy). If you are using snow peas, add them during the final 5 minutes of cooking.

4. Drizzle the sesame oil over the ingredients, give everything a final stir, and serve the casserole hot.

Preparation time: 1 hour to soak the dried ingredients, 15 minutes to assemble ingredients

Cooking time: 40 minutes

Serves: 2 as a main course, 4 to 6 as part of a Chinese meal.

SPICY SCALLOPS, HAM, AND VEGETABLES

This casserole has a rather soupy consistency and a mildly hot taste. If you do not care for hotness and pungency, omit the dried chili pepper and ginger root.

Ingredients

Lettuce to line casserole
¼ pound green beans, trimmed and cut into 2-inch pieces
½ pound scallops (if scallops are large, cut them in half)
3 slices boiled ham (2 to 3 ounces), cut into 2-by-1-inch slices ⅛ inch thick
¼ pound thin egg noodles, cooked and drained
¼ pound fresh mushrooms, cut into ¼-inch slices
½ can baby corn (15-ounce can), drained and rinsed

Braising Liquid

2 tablespoons thin soy sauce
2 tablespoons sherry
½ teaspoon sugar
2 cloves garlic, peeled and flattened
1 slice fresh ginger root, ⅛-inch thick, flattened
2 tablespoons hoisin sauce
1 dried chili pepper, broken in half (use both pod and seeds)
½ cup chicken broth

Final Seasoning

¼ teaspoon sesame oil
½ teaspoon thin soy sauce (or to taste)

Instructions

1. Line a 1½-quart casserole with lettuce leaves (see page 25). Sprinkle the green beans over the lettuce leaves.

2. Put the scallps on top of the green beans and the ham on top of the scallops. Then put the noodles on top of the ham and the mushrooms and corn on top of the noodles.

3. Mix the braising liquid ingredients well, and pour the liquid over the contents of the casserole. Bring the liquid to a boil over medium-high heat. Then reduce the heat to medium low, cover the casserole, and simmer the contents for ½ hour.

4. Stir all the ingredients, cover the casserole, and cook the combination pot for 15 minutes. Then discard the slice of ginger.

5. Drizzle the sesame oil over the ingredients, and add the soy sauce. Then give everything a final stir, and serve the combination pot hot.

Preparation time: 10 to 15 minutes
Cooking time: 45 minutes
Serves: 2 to 3

SCALLOPS, CHINESE SAUSAGE, AND BROCCOLI

The whiteness of the scallops, the red of the sausage, and the bright green of the broccoli make this a pretty dish to look at, and the combination of tastes and textures make it an even better one to eat.

Ingredients

Lettuce leaves to line casserole
½ pound scallops (if scallops are very large, cut them in half; otherwise leave them whole)
2 Chinese sausages, cut diagonally into ¼-inch slices
About ¼ cup sliced bamboo shoots
½ pound broccoli, cut into flowerets, stems peeled and cut into 2-by-1-by-⅛-inch slices

Braising Liquid (see Note)

1 tablespoon black soy sauce
1 tablespoon sherry
1 tablespoon oyster sauce
1 teaspoon sugar

Final Seasoning

¼ teaspoon sesame oil

Instructions

1. Line a 1-quart casserole with the lettuce leaves (see page 25).

2. Spread the scallops and Chinese sausage on top of the lettuce leaves. Then spread the bamboo shoots and broccoli flowerets and stems on top of everything.

3. Mix the braising liquid ingredients in a cup, stirring until the sugar is dissolved. Pour the liquid over the food in the casserole. Bring the liquid to a boil over high heat. Reduce the heat to medium low, cover the casserole, and simmer the contents for 50 to 60 minutes. (The broccoli will cook by steaming over the other ingredients. How crunchy you want your broccoli will determine the cooking time: less for crunch, more for mush.)

4. Drizzle the sesame oil over the food, and give all the ingredients a final stir. Discard the lettuce if you do not like the way it looks. Serve the combination pot hot.

Preparation time: 10 minutes or less
Cooking time: 50 to 60 minutes
Serves: 2

Note: The braising liquid ingredients may seem skimpy, but the water from the lettuce leaves increases the volume of liquid as the combination pot cooks.

DRIED OYSTERS, BARBECUED PORK, AND CHICKEN

If you cannot get either fresh or the dried oysters for this recipe (they can be interchanged), substitute a tin of smoked oysters, rinsing them well of the oil they are packed in. If you don't like oysters, substitute some other seafood, such as scallops, shrimp, squid, or fish fillets.

Ingredients

15 small dried oysters or the same number of fresh oysters
4   dried black Oriental mushrooms
    Lettuce leaves to line casserole
1   small onion, cut in half from top to bottom, peeled, and cut into ¼-inch slices along the grain
2   chicken legs (drumsticks and thighs), skinned, boned, and cut into 1-inch chunks
¼   pound barbecued pork, cut into ¼-inch slices (see page 168)
6   water chestnuts, cut in half

Braising Liquid

1   tablespoon thin soy sauce
1   tablespoon sherry
½   teaspoon sugar
2   cloves garlic, crushed
1   whole star anise

Final Seasoning

¼   teaspoon sesame oil

Instructions

1. Cover the dried oysters (if used) with water and soak them for 24 hours, changing the water twice. Drain the oysters.

2. Cover the mushrooms with warm water, and soak them for 1 hour. Drain them, remove and discard the stems, and cut the caps into quarters.

3. Line a 2-quart casserole with the lettuce leaves (see page 25). Sprinkle the onion slices over lettuce. Put the soaked oysters (or fresh oysters, or rinsed smoked oysters) on top of the lettuce and onions.

4. Mix the braising liquid ingredients in a cup, stirring until sugar is dissolved. Pour the liquid over the oysters. Bring the liquid to a simmer over medium heat. Reduce the heat to medium low, cover the casserole, and simmer the contents for 50 minutes.

5. Add the chicken, barbecued pork, mushrooms, and water chestnuts to the casserole and simmer all the ingredients for another 20 minutes.

6. Drizzle the sesame oil over food, give everything a final stir, and serve the casserole hot.

Preparation time: 24 hours to soak dried oysters; 1 hour to soak the mushrooms
Cooking time: About 1 hour
Serves: 2 as a main dish, 4 as part of a Chinese meal

DRIED OYSTERS, VEGETABLES, AND WALNUTS IN LETTUCE CUPS

The following recipe is for my version of a regional delicacy from the birthplace of the founder of the Chinese Republic, Dr. Sun Yat Sen. When I was a small child, my mother showed me a letter of thanks that my father had received from Dr. Sun Yat Sen for his part in casting off the symbol of repression imposed on Chinese men under the Manchu dynasty: the queue (pigtail) that they were required to wear as an outward sign of allegiance. My father's contribution was his cutting off the queues of the men in his village. At that age, I did not know who Dr. Sun Yat Sen was, and I did not think it was terribly important that my father had gone around cutting off pigtails. I know better now, and I salute him.

Ingredients

15   dried oysters
1   pound minced pork
6   dried black Oriental mushrooms
½   cup water chestnuts
½   cup bamboo shoots
1   cup fresh peas (or frozen peas, thawed)
½   cup walnuts, coarsely chopped
    Vegetable oil for browning oysters, pork, and vegetables

Marinade

4   teaspoons thin soy sauce
4   teaspoons sherry
½   teaspoon sugar
¼   teaspoon sesame oil
⅛   teaspoon finely grated fresh ginger root

Braising Liquid

2	teaspoons thin soy sauce
1	tablespoon sherry
½	teaspoon sugar
½	cup reserved oyster-soaking liquid (see Step 3)
2	tablespoons oyster sauce

Binder

2	teaspoons cornstarch
2	teaspoons cold water

Final Seasoning

¼	teaspoon sesame oil

Lettuce Cups

Crisp lettuce, several leaves per person, rinsed and thoroughly drained

Instructions

1. Cover the oysters with water and soak them for 24 hours, changing the water twice. Drain the oysters, reserving the water from the final soak. Cut the oysters into ½-inch dice.

2. Mix the marinade for the pork, and blend the meat and marinade well. Let it stand at room temperature for 1 hour.

3. Put the dried mushrooms to soak in warm water for 1 hour. Drain, stem (discard stems), and cut the mushrooms into ¼-inch dice. Cut the water chestnuts into ¼-inch dice; dice the bamboo shoots into pieces of the same size. Measure out the peas and walnuts.

4. Put a wok or a frying pan over high heat, and pour in enough oil to film it (about 1½ tablespoons), tilting the pan to coat the entire cooking surface. When the oil is hot, add the oysters, mushrooms, and marinated pork. Sauté the ingredients for a few minutes over medium heat until the pork is browned, stirring them a few times.

5. Mix the braising liquid ingredients in a 2-quart casserole,

and add the oyster and pork mixture to the casserole. Bring the liquid to a boil over high heat; then reduce the heat to medium low, cover the casserole, and simmer the oysters and pork for 15 minutes.

6. Add the water chestnuts, bamboo shoots, peas, and walnuts. Cover the casserole, and simmer its contents for another 15 minutes.

7. Stir the cornstarch and water to make the binder, and mix it into the braising liquid. Cook the sauce for a few minutes to allow it to thicken slightly.

8. Stir in the sesame oil.

9. Serve the stew hot, accompanied by a platter of crisp lettuce leaves. Put some of the mixture in the center of a leaf, and roll it up or fold it over.

Preparation time: 24 hours to soak the oysters; 1 hour to marinate the pork
Cooking time: 30 minutes
Serves: 3 or 4 as a main course, 6 to 8 as part of a Chinese meal

RICE-BASED CASSEROLES AND CONGEE

To the Chinese people, rice is a symbol of life itself. Chinese usually greet each other by asking whether they have eaten rice that day. A person who has lost his job has "had his rice bowl broken." The expression for eating a meal is "to eat rice." To spill rice deliberately is to insult someone in the strongest manner possible. A quotation from Cheng Pan-Cho, a well-known scholar of the Ching dynasty, illustrates the reverence the Chinese have toward rice:

Cutting stalks at noon time,
Perspiration drips to the earth,
Know you that your bowl of rice,
Each grain from hardship comes?

When I was a child, I was constantly admonished not to waste any rice and told that every grain left in my rice bowl represented a pockmark on the face of my future mate. All the children in the family, in order of seniority, had to ask the adults to "eat rice" before the meal began — a Chinese equivalent of saying grace.

The main reason some Westerners feel hungry after a Chinese meal is that they do not eat as much of the rice served with it as Chinese would eat. Rice is the principal part of the meal; meat and vegetables accompany the rice, rather than the other way around.

It is believed that rice came from India, as the name of one well-known kind, Patna, suggests. Rice worked its way to China and now is synonymous with its cuisine. I remember my tiny aunt and mother struggling with hundred-pound sacks of rice labeled <u>Texas Patna long-grain rice</u> that they had to empty into the metal rice bin.

A number of the recipes in this chapter (including Ground Beef Rice Casserole, Chicken and Chinese Sausage Rice Pot, and Clam Rice Pot) are typical of family-style cooking: Meat or fish and vegetables are cooked on top of the rice, thus saving on fuel and imparting delicious flavors to the rice.

Congee is another versatile dish. It is often eaten for breakfast, or as a light snack. Congee is also fed to invalids because it is such a bland dish and because the long cooking process makes it especially easy to digest.

EASY CLAM RICE POT

This meal-in-a-pot is so simple to make that it is suitable for someone living alone. What is not eaten the first day can be reheated the following day.

Ingredients

1½ cups raw long-grain rice
    6½-ounce can minced clams
1   teaspoon thin soy sauce
1   teaspoon sherry
½   teaspoon sesame oil
1   cup frozen peas

Instructions

1. Wash the rice (see Rice Chinese Style, page 28), drain it, and put it into a 2- or 2½-quart casserole. Add the minced clams, including their liquid. Stir the soy sauce, sherry, and sesame oil into the pot; then add enough water to get the one-thumb-knuckle measure (¾-inch) of liquid over the top of the rice.

2. Bring the liquid to a boil over high heat. Then reduce the heat to the lowest setting, and cook the ingredients for 10 minutes. Sprinkle the frozen peas into the casserole, cover the casserole again, and cook the rice pot for another 10 to 15 minutes, or until the peas are done. Serve the rice pot hot.

Preparation time: 5 minutes to wash the rice
Cooking time: 20 to 25 minutes
Serves: 2 or 3 as a main course, 6 as part of a Chinese meal

RICE POT WITH CHICKEN AND CHINESE SAUSAGE

This particular dish was a favorite in my family whenever there were large gatherings of relatives. I have adjusted the quantities for a smaller number of people.

Marinade

2   tablespoons thin soy sauce
2   tablespoons sherry
¼   teaspoon sugar
1   clove of garlic, peeled and finely minced
⅛   teaspoon grated fresh ginger root
¼   teaspoon sesame oil
⅛   teaspoon white pepper (optional)

Other Ingredients

½   frying chicken (about 1½ pounds), cut into small pieces (see page 36)
2   cups raw long-grain rice
3   Chinese sausages, cut into ⅛-inch diagonal slices

Garnish

2   scallions, cut into ¼-inch rounds (use both white and green parts)
     Chinese parsley (optional)

Instructions

1. Stir the marinade ingredients until sugar dissolves. Pour the marinade over the chicken, mixing to coat the meat well, and marinate the chicken for 1 hour at room temperature, turning the pieces over once or twice.

2. Wash the rice as directed for cooking Rice Chinese Style (see page 28). Put into a 2- or 3-quart casserole and add water to cover the rice by ¾ inch.

3. Lay the pieces of chicken on top of the rice, and pour in any extra marinade. Cover the pot, and bring the rice to a boil. Then reduce the heat to the lowest setting, and add the Chinese sausage. Cover the pot again, and cook the ingredients for 20 to 25 minutes. (Do not uncover the pot during this time.) Sprinkle the scallions and a few leaves of Chinese parsley on top, and serve the rice pot hot.

Preparation time: 1 hour
Cooking time: About ½ hour
Serves: 4 to 6

CHINESE PAELLA

This is a good dish to make if you are expecting a crowd for dinner. Served with a tossed salad, it should feed ten people easily. If the Chinese sausage and barbecued pork are unavailable, make substitutions of your choice, such as smoked ham or hot sausage, or both.

Marinade

2   tablespoons thin soy sauce
2   tablespoons sherry
½   teaspoon sugar
2   cloves garlic, peeled and finely minced
⅛   teaspoon grated fresh ginger root
½   teaspoon sesame oil

Other Ingredients

1   whole chicken breast, boned and cut into 1-inch chunks
½   pound shrimp, peeled and deveined
3   cups raw long-grain rice
3   Chinese sausages, cut into ⅛-inch-thick slices
1   dozen littleneck clams in the shell, scrubbed clean of sand
½   pound Chinese barbecued pork, cut into slices ⅛-inch thick (see page 168)
1   cup frozen peas

Final Seasoning

½   teaspoon sesame oil

Instructions

1. Stir the marinade ingredients together until the sugar is dissolved. Put the chicken and shrimp in separate bowls, and pour half the marinade over each. Marinate the chicken and shrimp for 1 hour at room temperature.

2. Meanwhile, wash the rice, and prepare it for cooking (see Rice Chinese Style, page 28). Make sure you use a casserole large enough (4 quarts or larger) to hold the rice, shellfish, and meats.

3. Cover the casserole, and bring the rice to a boil. As soon as the rice reaches the boiling point, add the chicken, shrimp, Chinese sausage, clams, and barbecued pork on top of the rice. Cover the pot, and cook the casserole over the lowest heat for 15 minutes. Sprinkle in the peas, and cook for another 10 to 15 minutes, or longer if all the clams have not opened.

4. Drizzle the sesame oil on top, give everything a final stir, and serve the paella hot.

Preparation time: 1 hour
Cooking time: 40 to 45 minutes
Serves: 8 to 10

TRIPLE-DRAGON RICE CASSEROLE

The three dragons in this recipe are small quantities of chicken livers, shrimp, and barbecued pork. If your fish man does not want to sell you less than half a pound of shrimp, freeze the quarter pound not needed for this recipe and use it some other time.

Marinade

1   tablespoon thin soy sauce
2   tablespoons sherry
2   tablespoons oyster sauce
¼   teaspoon sugar
1   clove garlic, peeled and finely minced
⅛   teaspoon grated fresh ginger root
¼   teaspoon sesame oil

Other Ingredients

6   chicken livers, trimmed and cut in half
¼   pound raw shrimp, peeled and deveined
2   cups raw long-grain rice
¼   pound Chinese barbecued pork, sliced ⅛ inch thick (see page 168)
4   water chestnuts, sliced ⅛ inch thick
    Handful of snow peas (about 6) cut in half on the diagonal

Instructions

1. Stir the marinade ingredients until the sugar has dissolved. Put the chicken livers and shrimp in separate bowls, pour half of the marinade over each, mix to coat them well, and marinate 1 hour at room temperature.

2. Meanwhile, wash the rice, and prepare it for cooking (see Rice Chinese Style, page 28) in a 3-quart casserole.

3. Cover the casserole, and bring the rice to a boil over high heat. As soon as the rice has reached the boiling point, reduce the heat to the lowest setting, and place the chicken livers and their marinade on top of the rice. Cover the casserole, and cook the chicken livers for 5 minutes. Add the shrimp and their marinade, and cook them for 10 minutes. Finally, add the barbecued pork, water chestnuts, and snow peas, and cook all the ingredients for another 5 minutes. Serve the rice pot hot.

Preparation time: 1 hour
Cooking time: 25 to 30 minutes
Serves: 4

EIGHT-JEWEL RICE CASSEROLE

This rice dish can be eaten with a salad or a vegetable to make a simple meal, or it can be served as an elegant accompaniment for meat or poultry (see Pot-Roasted Turkey, page 226). It also makes a wonderful stuffing for a turkey. The eight jewels are the chestnuts, Chinese sausage, mushrooms, onions, bamboo shoots, ham, water chestnuts and rice. You can substitute other jewels of your choosing, such as barbecued pork, shrimp, or chicken livers.

Ingredients

12 dried chestnuts
4   dried black Oriental mushrooms
2½ cups raw long-grain rice
    Vegetable oil for sautéing eight jewels
2   sweet Chinese sausages, cut into ¼-inch dice
1   large onion, peeled and cut into ¼-inch dice
¼   cup bamboo shoots, cut into ¼-inch dice
¼   cup water chestnuts, cut into ¼-inch dice
¼   cup smoked ham, cut into ¼-inch dice

Seasonings

1   tablespoon thin soy sauce
1   tablespoon sherry
1   tablespoon oyster sauce
¼   teaspoon sugar
¼   teaspoon white pepper
¼   teaspoon sesame oil
¼   to ½ cup mushroom-soaking liquid (see step 2)

Instructions

1. Cover the dried chestnuts with water, refrigerate, and soak them for 24 hours. Drain the chestnuts, cover them with fresh water, and simmer them for 1 hour. When the chestnuts are cool enough to handle, cut them into ¼-inch dice.

2. Cover the dried mushrooms with warm water, and soak them for 1 hour. Drain the mushrooms, reserving the liquid. Cut off and discard the stems; then cut the mushroom caps into ¼-inch dice.

3. Wash the rice (see Rice Chinese Style, page 28), drain it, and put it into a 3-quart casserole.

4. Put a frying pan over medium-high heat, and add enough oil to coat the bottom of the pan (about 1 tablespoon), tilting the pan to coat the entire cooking surface. When the oil is hot, add the chestnuts, mushrooms, sausages, onion, bamboo shoots, water chestnuts, and ham, and sauté them until the onions are translucent. Then add all the seasonings, and mix well.

5. Pour the contents of the frying pan into the rice pot, and mix the ingredients well with the rice. Add all the mushroom liquid; then add enough cold water to make the liquid level meet the thumb-knuckle test (¾ inch over the top of the rice).

6. Cover the pot, and bring the rice to a boil over high heat. Then reduce the heat to the lowest setting, and cook the eight-jewel rice 20 to 25 minutes, or until it is done. Mix the rice and jewels well, and serve the rice pot hot.

Preparation time: 24 hours for soaking the dried chestnuts; 1 hour for cooking them
Cooking time: 20 to 25 minutes
Serves: 4 to 6

CURRIED BEEF AND LIMA BEAN RICE POT

The amount of curry called for in this recipe is enough to let you know that it is there, but the dish is not especially spicy. Adjust the seasonings according to your own taste.

Marinade

2 tablespoons thin soy sauce
2 tablespoons sherry
½ teaspoon sugar
2 cloves garlic, peeled and finely minced
⅛ teaspoon grated fresh ginger root
½ teaspoon sesame oil
2 tablespoons curry powder (or to taste)
½ teaspoon chili powder
2 tablespoons tomato catsup

Other Ingredients

1½ pounds beef (skirt steak, chuck fillet, sirloin, or flank), sliced into pieces ¼ inch thick, 1 inch wide, and 2 inches long
2 cups raw long-grain rice
10-ounce box frozen lima beans, defrosted

Final Seasoning

½ teaspoon sesame oil

Instructions

1. Mix the marinade ingredients in a cup, stirring until the sugar has dissolved. Pour the marinade over the beef, and stir well to make sure that all the slices are well coated. Marinate the beef for at least 1 hour at room temperature.

2. Meanwhile, prepare the rice for cooking (see Rice Chinese Style, page 28), making sure you use a pot large enough (3½ to 4 quarts), to hold the rice, which will at least double in bulk when cooked, beef, and lima beans. Add enough water to cover the rice by ¾ inch (the thumb-knuckle test), and begin cooking the rice over high heat.

3. Bring the rice to a boil. Then immediately reduce the heat to the lowest setting. Mix the beef and its marinade with the lima beans, place the mixture on top of the rice, cover the pot, and cook the casserole for 10 minutes.

4. Stir the beef and lima beans into the rice. Cover the casserole again, and cook all the ingredients for an additional 15 to 20 minutes, until the beef, beans, and rice are done.

5. Drizzle the sesame oil over the dish, give everything a final stir, and serve the rice pot hot.

Preparation time: 1 hour
Cooking time: About 40 to 45 minutes
Serves: 6

RICE POT WITH GROUND BEEF

When I was a little girl, my family thought I was pretty scrawny and would cook all kinds of things to strengthen my blood and add some meat to my bones. My mother frequently made a kind of beef tea. She would put a piece of beefsteak mixed with some brown beans and water in a special porcelain jar with a fitted, domed lid and fitted metal trivet and place the jar in a large pot containing a few inches of water that was brought first to a boil, then to a simmer. The pot was covered, and the meat was cooked for several hours. The juices extracted in the jar were what I had to drink. I hated beef tea then, but I think I would love it now. This casserole of ground beef and rice makes me think of that beef tea.

Ingredients

4   dried black Oriental mushrooms
½   pound ground beef
2   cups raw long-grain rice
5   water chestnuts, cut into ¼-inch dice
¼   cup bamboo shoots, cut into ¼-inch dice
¼   to ½ cup mushroom-soaking liquid (see step 1)
½   cup frozen peas

Marinade

4   teaspoons thin soy sauce
4   teaspoons sherry
¼   teaspoon sugar
⅛   teaspoon grated fresh ginger root
¼   teaspoon sesame oil

Instructions

1. Cover the mushrooms with warm water, and soak them for 1 hour. Drain the mushrooms, reserving the soaking liquid. Remove and discard the stems, and cut the caps into ¼-inch dice.

2. Meanwhile, mix the marinade ingredients together, stirring until the sugar is dissolved. Blend the marinade well with the ground beef, and let the mixture stand for 1 hour at room temperature.

3. Wash the rice, and have it ready to cook Chinese style (see page 28) in a 2-quart casserole.

4. Mix the water chestnuts, bamboo shoots, diced mushrooms, and mushroom-soaking liquid into the beef, and mix to blend all the ingredients well.

5. Cover the casserole, and bring the rice to a boil over high heat. Reduce the heat to the lowest setting, and add the frozen peas. Cook the rice and peas for 5 minutes. Then add the beef mixture, with its marinade, on top of the rice. Cook all the ingredients for another 15 to 20 minutes. Give everything a final stir, and serve the rice pot hot.

Preparation time: About 1 hour
Cooking time: 20 to 30 minutes
Serves: 6

RICE POT WITH SQUID AND BARBECUED PORK

Squid is not to everyone's liking, and cleaning it can be a messy business. Unfortunately, because it is such a time-consuming job, the fish monger usually will not do it for you. The first time I ever had to deal with squid — other than eating it — I was working in an Italian restaurant in Provincetown and had to clean twenty pounds of squid. (You learn quickly when you are dealing with that amount.) Occasionally, you can purchase frozen squid that are already cleaned.

Marinade

2 tablespoons thin soy sauce
2 tablespoons sherry
¼ teaspoon sugar
1 clove garlic, peeled and finely minced
⅛ teaspoon grated fresh ginger root
¼ teaspoon sesame oil

Other Ingredients

½ pound squid, cleaned and cut into ½-inch slices (leave the tentacles whole)
2 cups raw long-grain rice
¼ pound Chinese barbecued pork, cut into ⅛-inch slices (see page 168)

Instructions

1. Stir the marinade ingredients together until the sugar dissolves. Pour the mixture over squid, stirring to coat it thoroughly, and marinate it for ½ hour at room temperature.

2. Wash the rice, and prepare it for cooking (see Rice Chinese Style, page 28) in a 2- or 2½-quart casserole.

3. Cover the casserole, and bring the rice to a boil over high heat. Reduce the heat to the lowest setting, and cook the rice for 5 minutes.

4. Arrange the squid slices on top of the rice, and cook them for 15 minutes. Add the barbecued pork, and cook all the ingredients for another 5 minutes. Serve the rice pot hot.

Preparation time: About 45 minutes
Cooking time: 25 to 30 minutes
Serves: 4

RICE WITH SCALLOPS

This dish somewhat resembles Rice with Gingered Oysters. If you wish, you can omit the ginger.

Marinade

4   teaspoons thin soy sauce
4   teaspoons sherry
¼   teaspoon sugar
1   clove garlic, peeled and finely minced
⅛   teaspoon grated fresh ginger root (optional)
¼   teaspoon sesame oil

Other Ingredients

½   pound scallops (if scallops are large, cut them in half)
1½ cups raw long-grain rice

Garnish

1   scallion, cut into ¼-inch rounds (use both green and white parts) (optional)

Instructions

1. Mix the marinade ingredients, stirring until the sugar has dissolved, and pour the mixture over the scallops. Stir the scallops so that they are well coated, and marinate them for ½ hour at room temperature.

2. Wash the rice, and have it ready to cook (see Rice Chinese Style, page 28) in a 2- or 2½-quart casserole.

3. Cover the casserole, and bring the rice to a boil over high heat. Reduce the heat to the lowest setting, and cook the rice for 10 minutes.

4. Arrange the scallops on top of the rice, cover the casserole again, and cook the ingredients for 15 minutes, or until the scallops are done. Sprinkle the scallion rounds on top of the scallops, and serve the casserole hot.

Preparation time: 30 minutes
Cooking time: 25 to 30 minutes
Serves: 4 or 5

OYSTER SAUCE BEEF AND GREEN BEAN RICE POT

Oyster Sauce Beef is usually a stir-fried dish, but there is a way of cooking it at the same time that you are cooking your rice: Simply put the beef mixture on top of the rice. You save on fuel and avoid last-minute fussing. With the addition of green beans this becomes a one-pot dinner.

Marinade

1	tablespoon thin soy sauce
2	tablespoons sherry
¼	teaspoon sugar
2	cloves garlic, peeled and finely minced
⅛	teaspoon grated fresh ginger root
½	teaspoon sesame oil
	Pinch of white pepper
3	tablespoons oyster sauce

Beef

1½ pounds beef (skirt steak, chuck fillet, sirloin, or flank), sliced into pieces ¼-inch thick, 1-inch wide, and 2-inches long

Green Beans

1 pound green beans, trimmed and cut into 2-inch lengths

Rice

2 cups raw long-grain rice

Final Seasoning

½ teaspoon sesame oil

Instructions

1. Mix the marinade ingredients, stirring them until sugar dissolves. Pour the marinade over the beef slices, mixing well to coat the meat thoroughly. Let sit for at least 1 hour at room temperature.

2. Drop the beans into a large pot of boiling water, and let them boil for 4 minutes. Drain the beans, cool them under running cold water, and drain the beans again.

3. Follow instructions for cooking Rice Chinese Style (see page 28), making sure you use a pot large enough (3¼ to 4 quarts) to hold the rice (which will double in bulk when cooked), beef, and green beans. When the rice has come to the first boil, immediately reduce the heat to the lowest setting. Mix the beef and its marinade with green beans, and put them on top of the rice. Cover the pot and simmer the ingredients for 10 minutes.

4. Stir the beef and green beans into the rice. Cover the pot, and cook the ingredients for an additional 15 minutes, or until the beef is done.

5. Drizzle on the sesame oil, give everything a final stir, and serve the rice pot hot.

Preparation time: 1 hour to marinate the beef
Cooking time: 35 to 40 minutes
Serves: 6

RICE WITH GINGERED OYSTERS

Fish markets sell tins of fresh, shucked oysters that make this an easy dish to prepare.

Marinade

4   teaspoons thin soy sauce
4   teaspoons sherry
¼   teaspoon sugar
1   clove garlic, peeled and finely minced
¼   teaspoon grated fresh ginger root
¼   teaspoon sesame oil

Other Ingredients

½-pint fresh oysters (about 12 oysters)
1½ cups raw long-grain rice

Garnish

1   scallion, cut into ¼-inch rounds (use both green and white parts) (optional)

Instructions

1. Mix the marinade ingredients, stirring until the sugar has dissolved, and pour the mixture over the oysters. Stir the oysters so that they are well coated, and marinate them for ½ hour at room temperature.

2. Wash the rice, and have it ready to cook (see Rice Chinese Style, page 28) in a 2- to 2½-quart casserole.

3. Cover the pot, and bring the rice to a boil over high heat. Then reduce the heat to the lowest setting, and cook the rice for 10 minutes.

4. Place the oysters on top of the rice, cover the casserole, and cook the ingredients for another 15 minutes, or until the oysters are done. Sprinkle the scallion rounds on top, and serve the casserole hot.

Preparation time: 30 minutes
Cooking time: 25 to 30 minutes
Serves: 4 or 5

SHRIMP-IN-THE-SHELL RICE POT

My aunt and my mother always cooked shrimp with the shells on. I swear that shrimp cooked that way have much more taste. This is a dish that you really have to dig into with your fingers to peel the shells off. It gets a little messy, but it is worth the effort.

Marinade

1	teaspoon thin soy sauce
1	teaspoon sherry
¼	teaspoon sugar
	Pinch of white pepper
¼	teaspoon sesame oil
1	clove garlic, peeled and finely minced
⅛	teaspoon grated fresh ginger root
1	teaspoon tomato catsup

Other Ingredients

½	pound shrimp, shells cut open along the back and deveined (leave shells in place)
1	cup raw long-grain rice

Instructions

1. Mix the marinade ingredients, stirring until the sugar dissolves. Pour the liquid over the shrimp, stirring to coat them well, and marinate the shrimp for 1 hour at room temperature.

2. Cook the rice Chinese Style in a 2-quart casserole over high heat (see page 28).

3. During the last 10 to 12 minutes of cooking the rice, add the shrimp and any marinade remaining in the bowl on top of the rice. Cover the casserole, and cook the ingredients until the shrimp and rice are done (10 to 15 minutes). Serve the rice pot hot.

Preparation time: 1 hour
Cooking time: 20 to 30 minutes
Serves: 2 or 3

Note: For a spicier variation, add 1 teaspoon curry powder and a dash of chili powder to the marinade.

CONGEE (JOOK)

For some obscure reason, the Chinese rice porridge dish that is called jook in Cantonese is known in the United States and Great Britain as congee, an Anglo-Indian term meaning "water in which rice has been boiled." Few Westerners know of this dish, which is very typical of Chinese home-style cooking. Congee is often eaten for breakfast or as a light snack at any time of the day, including midnight, and is a very inexpensive way of stretching rice.

Basically, a small amount of rice is cooked with a large amount of water for several hours. The rice grains absorb so much water that they explode and thicken the water to a porridgelike consistency. Congee is flavored with whatever garnish or condiment you wish: raw fish slices cooked in the heat of the congee, ground beef, slices of thousand-year-old eggs, hard-cooked salted duck eggs, pickled ginger, sweet radish, roasted nuts, white bean curd cheese, pickled cucumber, scallions, fresh coriander or Chinese parsley, pieces of roast duck, pieces of pig's stomach, of kidneys, shreds of raw lettuce, and on and on. The list is endless.

This version of jook is richer than some because chicken broth is used instead of plain water.

Ingredients

1   cup long-grain rice
2   quarts chicken broth (or 1 quart water and 1 quart broth)
    Salt and pepper to taste (optional)
    Garnish of your choice

Instructions

1. Wash the rice until the water runs clear (see Rice Chinese Style, page 28). Mix the rice with the chicken broth in a 3½- or 4-quart pot or casserole. Bring the broth to a boil, reduce the heat to medium low, cover the pot, and simmer the rice for 2½ hours, stirring the rice occasionally to keep it from sticking to the bottom of the pot, where it might scorch or form a crust.

2. The consistency of the <u>jook</u> is up to the individual; just as oatmeal or farina can be on the thick or thin side, so can <u>jook</u>. If the mixture seems too thick, thin it with more broth or water.

3. Add salt and pepper to taste, or leave the congee to be seasoned at the table by the diners, who will also garnish it according to their own desires.

Preparation time: 10 minutes to wash the rice
Cooking time: 2½ hours
Serves: 4 to 6

INDEX